Yves B

# VERDUN

## Historical
## and
## tourist guide

YSEC

# Other English Books about Verdun and its area published by Ysec Editions :

**Douaumont Ossuary**
Olivier Gérard & Jean-Luc Kaluzko
ISBN : 9-782846-731980

**Verdun, le champ de bataille vu du ciel**
(Verdun, the battlefield seen from the sky)
Jean-Luc Kaluzko
ISBN : 9-782846-731249

**Cover Picture** : Fort Douaumont (Ysec Photo)
Maps devised by Angelica Labarre Copyright Ysec Editions.

# CONTENTS

## Historical guide

## Tourist guide

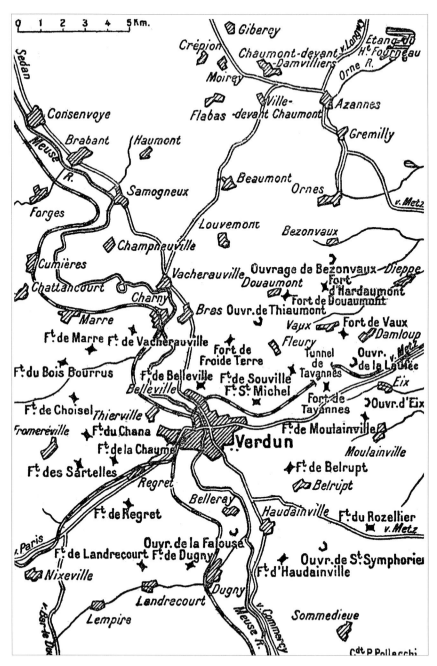

THE FORTIFIED AREA AROUND VERDUN AT THE BEGINNING
OF THE WAR

4

# VERDUN, A FRONTIER TOWN

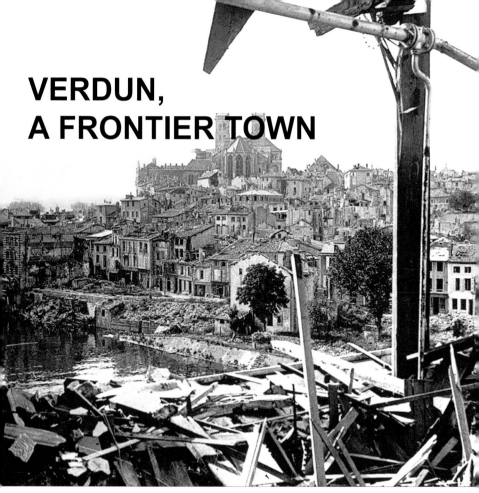

## The attempts at surrouding the town

In the aftermath of the defeat in 1870, France lost the Alsace, the German-speaking and some French-speaking areas of the Lorraine. Metz, the most important fortified town in eastern France thus became German. As a consequence, it became possible to invade France by the eastern frontier. In the 1880's, new defences were devised under the supervision of General Séré de Rivières, Head of Engineer in the Ministry of War. The defences concerned several towns close to the new frontier, including Verdun, Toul and Belfort.

The area stretching between Verdun and Germany, called "plaine de Woëvre", or Woëvre

*A view of Verdun in 1916. It is often said that the battle started with the explosion of a 380 mm shell which fell down on the front of the cathedral, on 21st February 1916. Although it was not considered a priority for the German artillery, Verdun was the target of many guns and civilians had to be evacuated. (Author's coll.)*

5

plain, did not lend itself well to defence. However, Verdun, located on rough terrain on the banks of the Meuse river, made an excellent entrenchment. Moreover, its location was capital for it prevented any invasion from the plains of Champagne. The loss of Verdun would have created a real threat for Paris and its region. That is why the Germans kept trying to capture the town during the first three years of the conflict.

When the war was declared, the French remained below the frontier. The 6th and 2nd Corps were ordered to keep their positions, respectively in the south of Verdun, on the Hauts-de-Meuse and on the Meuse river , downstream from Verdun.

During the days following the outbreak of the war, the Germans kept making offensive reconnaissances on Woëvre plain. They culminated on 10th August with the skirmish of Mangiennes. It was a small village located 25km north of Verdun which was attacked by the 6. Kavallerie Division, the 124. I.R. and the 5. Jäger Bn, backed up by three batteries on horses and machine guns. On the French side, the area was occupied by the 91st R.I. and three artillery batteries (1st group of the A.D./4).

In the morning of 10th August, the covering 9th Brigade of Dragons, warned the defences in Mangiennes about the arrival of German troops. The battle began at 9 am with an artillery fire. At 3 pm, the German infantry attacked. They managed to reach the eastern border of Mangiennes and a French counter-attack, led by the 130th R.I. which had just arrived, was repelled with many casualties. But at 5.30 pm, the 91st R.I. counter-attacked, backed up by the artillery of the AD./4. The Germans were forced back with losses that were judged heavy by General Gerard : 200 dead and 400 wounded. The French celebrated their victory but, unfortunately, they were deluding themselves.

## A general withdrawal

When reports informed General Joffre, the Commander-in-chief of the French armies, that the German effort was gaining momentum in Belgium, he ordered the general offensive in the North, in order to defeat the Germans on Belgian territory: the 3rd and 4th French Armies had to strike the Germans on the right flank in order to isolate them from their bases of departure. The strategy was well-conceived. Unfortunately, Joffre did not know that the Germans had managed a real feat, that is to say, to line up all their reserve corps on the front line. The French thought they would encounter covering troops and scattered elements but were in fact confronted with two armies of twenty-two divisions in line.

*Some French soldiers taking up position in a hastily dug trench. Men reload their Lebel rifle, a weapon which proved inefficient in front of Maxim machine guns or Mauser rifles. (IWM)*

*Hidden behind a wall, a French foot soldier is firing at the German invader, in 1914. After the deadly setbacks of the battle of the frontiers, the French armies were forced to retreat everywhere. The phenomenon was less important around Verdun than in the North though. (IWM)*

The attack was frontal and quickly turned into a real disaster for the French. Thousands of French soldiers were killed by Maxim machine guns.

This French failure caused Joffre to order troops to fall back toward the South, in order to avoid an encirclement or a disruption of the plan. On the whole front, troops started to withdraw. At the beginning of September, the 3rd French army, led by General Sarrail, retreated toward Bar-Le-Duc but remained linked to the fortified area in Verdun. On the German side, the 5. Armee of the Imperial Crown Prince immediately followed the troops of Sarrail in order to take Bar-le-Duc and then surround Verdun.

## The counter-offensive

On 6th September 1914, the Crown Prince sent his divisions toward the South, on the very same day when Joffre ordered the general counter-offensive of the French army on the whole front line. The frontal clash between the two armies was tremendous. The battles lasted for three days, without any real victory.

And yet, on 13th September, the Germans drew back. This dramatic turn of events was due to the victory of the Marne which suddenly changed the situation on a strategic level.

# Genevoix vs Rommel

The battle which took place during the night of 10th September 1914 in Vauxmarie had the astonishing particularity to oppose two men which were to become very famous after the war: Maurice Genevoix, future award winner of the Goncourt prize and member of the French Academy and Erwin Rommel future head of the Afrikakorps and Marshal of the Reich.

In September 1914, both had the same rank : Second Lieutenant. Both commanded a platoon and as luck would have it, they opposed each other in the battle of Vauxmarie. Their testimonies were gathered by G. Hauteclerc, in a review entitled *Revue Historique des Armées*. We can only quote short extracts here. " *The troop is anxiously waiting for the order to attack,* Rommel writes. *The men have been drenched to the bones and been shivering with cold for a long time now... At about 3 am, the order to attack is finally coming. In close ranks, the battalion is rushing down the slope with an extraordinary fury, dashing toward the enemy who occupied the railways and is defeating them. [...] Wherever he resists, the enemy is eliminated by the bayonet.*"

Genevoix, for whom the rain is not chilly but tepid, is surprised by the assailants rushing only 30 metres away. " *The muddy ground is shaking under the trampling of boots. We are going to be trampled, swept away, destroyed. We are barely sixty men [...] We shall not be able to hold out against the amazing pressure of all these ranks of men rushing on us like a herd of bulls [...] All the rifles of the section are firing all together. And I can see a huge void forming amidst the screaming crowd of men.*"

However, Genevoix and his men had to draw back under the pressure. Rommel and his troop set up in an advanced position, but at daybreak, the French artillery opened fire on them and the Germans were forced to leave their newly conquered position after only 36 hours. We can but highly recommend the reading of the wonderful books written by Maurice Genevoix, currently gathered under the title "*Ceux de 14*".

Then, the fate of these two men took different directions. Genevoix became famous for his war narratives and Rommel for his military deeds, more precisely those in Italy in 1917, without speaking about his career during the Second World War. Genevoix did everything to commemorate the memory of the soldiers of WWI, until his death at the beginning of the 1980's.

*The main entry of Fort Troyon a little before the battles in September 1914. It was built between 1877 and 1880 and resisted the German artillery fires. The fort also prevented the Bavarians from crossing the Meuse, which would have probably caused the fall of Verdun. (Le Hallé's coll.)*

During three days, the army of the Crown Prince headed for the North and stopped in the Aire valley, forming a line streching from Varennes-en-Argonne to Brabant-sur-Meuse. Despite many efforts, the 3rd French army could not overtake the German positions.

## The Bavarians offensive on Saint-mihiel

After the failure of the Marne, Moltke was replaced by Falkenhayn at the head of the armies. The latter was a much more methodical man. In order to outflank the French, he triggered the well-known race to the sea. At the same time, he took interest in Verdun which he decided to invade by the south-east. General Von Strantz was in charge of the assault : they wanted to capture the Hauts-de-Meuse and then walk on Saint-Mihiel, located along the stream of the Meuse river, 35 kilometres up Verdun. Strantz had two army corps to carry out the plan. On the other side, the 75th Division of reserve troops watched over the Hautsde Meuse. The division was composed of barely 7,500 exhausted men and had lost most of its leaders. In the morning of 20th September 1914, the German artillery started the battle. The infantry quickly followed but was confronted to an unexpected resistance from the French division. The fighting lasted for 48 long hours, which was the necessary time for the Bavarians to destroy the 75th D.I. Then, they rushed by forced marches toward the Meuse, without encountering one single obstacle. On the 23rd, they took Saint-Mihiel and even started forming a bridgehead on the left bank of the Meuse. The capture of the Fort called Camp des Romains on 25th September reinforced their position. But it would have been an illusion to think they could go on alone toward the East : the surrounding of Verdun by the South did not take place because the Prussians, who held the right flank of the Bavarians, were contained claiming a lot of lives, in Saint-Remy and in Spada. The Bavarian victory thus remained unconsummated.

*The entry of the Fort called Camp des Romains, photographed after the war. The fort suffered a lot during the battles in 1914. Its capture by the Germans allowed them to remain in Saint-Mihiel. (Le Hallé's coll.)*

# THE ARGONNE

The Argonne and its dense forest represented a major obstacle for military operations. Oriented from North to South and about six kilometres large, the Argonne formed a natural wall between the 4. and 5. Armee. When the Crown Prince decided to start the offensive on 20th September 1914 in order to complete the surrounding of Verdun by the West, his soldiers were marching through the Aire valley. The farther they marched, the more threatening the Argonne forest appeared to them.

Several patrols were sent into the forest and a few shots were exchanged with the French troops. The presence of the enemy urged the Crown Prince to set up a combined operation which was to allow the 16. Armee Korps led by von Mudra (5. Armee) to join the 27.I.D. (4. Armee) in the Bois de la Gruerie and thus gather both armies.

Both detachments started marching on 28th September. The journey through the forest was slow and dangerous. The enemy remained hidden until the last moment and a back up of the artillery was impossible. From the very first day, the Germans were bogged down. In an attempt to be the one to decide, von Mudra sent a battery of heavy mortars to his foot soldiers on the front line.

The 30th September began with a systematic bombing of the French positions but the thickness of the trees hindered vision and the German vanguards were more than 2,500 meters away from the Four-de-Paris at the end of the day. Their situation was all the more difficult since the French clung to the Hill 285.

As the Germans stopped marching, the French took advantage of it and decided to counter-attack on 2nd October, without success. On the 4th, the Germans attacked in their turn, mainly in the Bois de la Gruerie, around Bagatelle. Despite the extra reinforcement of Minenwerfer, the waves of German assaults were defeated in front of the French positions where areas of brushwood allowed to clear glacises.

To limit human losses, von Mudra ordered to progress by sapping, a tedious, methodical but life-saving operation. But the Prussian officers decided to smoke the French away. The first attempts with inflamed parcels of celluloid were not very successful. But on 5th October, the Germans attacked with Flamenwerfer, or flamethrowers. It was the very first time such a weapon was used. But the results were rather disappointing since the first French trench was not conquered before a week.

*The lack of trench mortars was a real plague for the French army throughout the first winter of the war. As a result, substitutes had to be found: in the reserves of old forts were stored old mortars for siege, dating back to king Louis-Philippe or Napoleon III. The one photographed below is a 15 cm piece from 1839. These weapons were used for want of anything better, before the arrival of the Crapouillot, a trench mortar.*
*(Author's coll.)*

On 13th October, von Mudra was appointed at the head of the war in the Argonne. Three divisions of infantry, two battalions of Jägers and many troops of engineers formed an autonomous force capable of succeeding in this mission, that is to say the conquest of a strong starting point in the Argonne from where they would be able to trigger future major operations. In mid-October 1914, the front was disorganised and trenches were scarce.

Von Mudra first renounced to disorganised attacks against French positions. Before striking, he decided to structure the rear front. In parallel, local commanders carried out a series of

*General Von Mudra in the Argonne forest. Much respected by his men because of his simplicity, he managed to organize the German front in the Argonne and his victories, though limited, were impressive. (Ysec's coll.)*

*Map of the western area of the Argonne forest, with the Bois de la Gruerie and the Four de Paris. (Ysec's coll.)*

operations in order to rectify the front line. Each attack followed the same pattern, first with a violent bombing by Minenwerfer, then a brief assault with grenades. Goals were limited but the French were gradually pushed back toward the South. Thus, on 1st December 1914, three trench lines were conquered, 241 soldiers were made prisoners, against only six German soldiers killed and sixteen wounded.

Although the German advance did not reach more than a kilometre, the morale of the 2nd French Corps was lower and lower. The Germans originated all the operations and their assaults were always successful. On the French side, the trenches had very poor facilities and the rear guard was really disorganized. Daily losses were heavy even when there was no fighting.

*German troops in a church in the Meuse countryside. For the Germans, the Argonne was synonymous with victory in 1915 and the troops liked this deep forest which reminded them of home. (IWM)*

2l cm Mörser in Feuerstellung

*A 21cm mortar in the Argonne forest. The German superiority on an artillery level was crushing in 1915 and the result was easy to guess : French troops were always on the defensive and could not keep up their position. (Ysec's coll.)*

## Offensives launched again

At the beginning of 1915, the Germans were ready to attack. At first, they tried to capture correct points of departure. On 7th and 8th January, 48 hours after an abortive French attack, a very strong assault was launched against the Ravin des Meurissons and the ridge named the Fille-Morte. In a few hours, more than 1,600 prisoners were captured. At the Ravin des Meurissons, the Germans advanced on more than 1,200 meters. The 46th Regiment was totally crushed.

Then, on 29th January, a tremendous attack caused a heavy toll for the French troops in the Bois de la Gruerie. They counter-attacked four times on that day but failed every time. It was a major failure which cost the lives of 2,476 men and 56 officers in the 40th D.I. On the German side, the toll was less heavy but important nonetheless. A prisoner declared: "We walked on the corpses of our men." Actually, the losses of the 27. I. D. amounted to about 900 men.

However, the Germans remained the ones in control.

Humbert explains the German success this way : *"(Our troops) occupy trenches which were devised as prior events were taking place and their improvised design is often defective when under the fire of the enemy. As the enemy is very close to us (about 30 meters away from here), those trenches have neither shelters nor barbwire networks. The garrisons could only manage to throw over the wall some chevaux-de-frise or hang some wire between the trees. Our artillery has much difficulty carrying out an efficient barrage fire because of the premature explosion in the trees."*

After the German success, a relative calm came back to the Argonne for the French tried to initiate offensives in the Aire valley, toward Boureuilles, Vauquois and Varennes.

*German soldiers are celebrating victory in 1915, somewhere in the Argonne forest. (IWM)*

# The battles during the summer

While the French offensive turned into a quagmire in the valley, Von Mudra prepared his summer attacks. On 20th June, he launched an assault which was but a strategic rehearsal of a major future action. Despite clear success, the death toll was heavy on both sides.

On 30th June, von Mudra struck with even stronger against the salient of Bagatelle. More than 120 pieces of artillery were packed in the area. The waves of assault used up 36,000 grenades! The Germans called the effect of these bombardments a Vernichtungsorgie (an orgy of destruction).

When the initial assault by the artillery was over, the French trenches had been levelled up, men buried alive or totally paralysed, phone lines had been cut off. At some point on the front line, the Germans managed to reach their objective of the day or even of the day after in one or two hours. The position in Bagatelle was the only one to resist, even though surrounded.

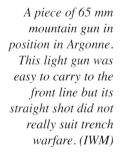

*A piece of 65 mm mountain gun in position in Argonne. This light gun was easy to carry to the front line but its straight shot did not really suit trench warfare. (IWM)*

The battle went on until 3rd July when von Mudra's soldiers finally controlled all their objectives. The Germans lost about 2,300 men, the French lost 8,500 men, including 2,500 prisoners.

For Joffre, this series of failures was unbearable. Although he did not give new means to Sarrail, he ordered "a counter-offensive in order not only to regain lost grounds but also to ensure moral superiority and rectify the situation." The assault was prepared with absolutely no ingenuity by Sarrail who decided to attack "right in front of him". But on 13th July, on the eve of the French attack, von Mudra struck again, even stronger than on 30th June. The violence of the bombing had never been seen before. Huge 305 mm shells smashed the earth open, buried the trenches, destroyed the shelters. In one of them, near the Ravin des Meurissons, the Germans found 108 corpses. The rear French positions were then drowned in poison gas. A real slaughter took place on the front line. The Hill 285, the

*A crossbow in 1915. For want of appropriate weapons, French soldiers often had to do with what they had at the beginning of the trench warfare. This crossbow, used to throw small grenades, was not very harmful but offered at least some moral comfort to the troops.*

*Another type of impro-vised trench mortar which looks more than basic and is surely a weapon of substitution. It was such a poor one, that it was quickly abandonned.*

cornerstone in the French defence, was taken. The whole front was about to fall apart.

The 66th Battalion of Chasseurs on foot of Vincennes was sent to regain the position. They started attacking with the sound of the bugle and entire ranks of chasseurs were killed. However, the Hill 285 was soon reached and then conserved.

Despite the terrible losses of 13th July , and although he had already used up a good deal of his ammunitions, Sarrail launched his offensive on 14th July. The exhausted troops could not achieve a breakthrough. Trapped under the shells, the troops were forced back to their starting points, leaving thousands of men behind, including 2,800 dead for the 1st Colonial Brigade. Such a failure caused Sarrail to suspend the assault. From 20th June to 20th July 1915, his 3rd Army lost 32,405 men! Despite censorship, such a disaster could not remain unheard by the public opinion, and Joffre decided to get rid of Sarrail who was replaced by General Humbert.

At the same time, the battles calmed down even if they started again in September. But von Mudra was no longer the sole master : the French offensive in the Champagne was serious enough to make it necessary to send there stronger artillery reinforcements, which were taken from close areas like the Argonne. As the year ended, the Germans started preparing their strongest offensive since 1914, and it would be launched against Verdun. Von Mudra played a major role in it. The phase of active warfare ended in the Argonne.

But it did not mean the battles stopped in this huge forest. The two adversaries started the mine warfare. It was indeed the end of huge assaults out in the open and the beginning of an underground and sly type of war. The craters that still can be seen today around Hill 285 illustrate this phenomenon.

VAUQUOIS

In Argonne, the French army could not afford to launch offensive operations. But in the Aire valley, a few kilometres east, the ground was better suited to infantry attacks. At the end of September 1914, the Germans set up on the heights that defended Varennes, above the valley. The highest one was composed of a village named Vauquois, located on top of a "Butte", a hillock. Any French progression toward the north-east was made impossible by the German occupation of Vauquois.

A first attempt failed on 28th and 29th October 1914. General Sarrail had apparently counted on creating a surprise since there was no artillery in front of Vauquois. The attack on the 28th was pushed back by German guns. On the day after, although the enemy had been warned against it, the French launched the exact same assault: without any artillery backup, foot soldiers lined up in the fields and attacked. It was a pointless slaughter.

*A revolver canon in Vauquois. This one is set up on the front line on top of the hillock, in order to directly shoot at German trenches opposite the French lines, in the ruins of the village that will soon entirely disappear under countless mine explosions.*
*(Ysec's coll.)*

# The assault
# of February 1915

Vauquois was calm again for several months. It was in the Argonne forest that battles intensified. Here is the point of view of General Sarrail : *"The Germans have clearly gained moral superiority. They attack whenever and wherever they want and they always succeed."*

Aware that the 32nd Corps could not gain morale supremacy back in Argonne, the head of the 3rd Army was willing nevertheless to quickly go back to action, mainly to comfort the troops. He planned an offensive in the Aire valley in which Hill 263, (on the border of the Argonne forest) Boureuilles and Vauquois were the first objectives from West to East.

Joffre agreed and the operation was planned for mid-February. The artillery was more than present this time since a battery of 200 mm howitzers and a battery of 270 mm guns reinforced the artillery of the 32nd and 15th Corps.

For the first time, mines were used in Vauquois. Ill-prepared, they just shook the walls of the German trenches.

Two infantry regiments started to attack at 12.45 pm. On the left, the 76th R.I. was immediately stopped by the machine guns of a flanking blockhouse which had avoided the artillery. On the right, despite several difficulties, the Cuny Battalion from the 31st R.I. *"manages nevertheless to partly enter Vauquois, to cross the village until the northern edge, to take the Germans by surprise and follow them while they flee. But, they were counter-attacked before being able to entirely enter the village by small and organised groups who rushed from East and West. Thus, they had to stop their advance and, at 1.30 pm, go back to their trenches, having lost many officers and bringing 6 prisoners with them."*

The slopes of the Éparges after the attack. The scene of desolation is the same in Vauquois where the French assailants had to climb a very steep slope to try to reach the German trenches of the first line. Sergeant Georges Boucheron recounts:
"From everywhere, dark blue greatcoats are rushing in. One step and they are all falling down : the Boches , who outnumber us, seem to be shooting from a hiding place: almost all bullets are aimed at heads; the groups are falling down one by one, in front of me […] I am jumping onto the top of a ditch and running onwards as fast as I can, as a new group is rushing out of the forest. I am running like a fool when a sudden pain is paralysing me. I am apsing. In front of me, a man is swaying from side to side, before collapsing with many other men. We all form a heap. Nobody is standing anymore. The shooting is raging on. There is a heavy weight on my legs. In front of my head, I can see a body lying on his back, he no longer moves. On my right, three soldiers seem to be hugging each other. On my left, I see a big fellow falling in a heap, a bullet entered the top of his skull : the man fell down like an ox that has been knocked out […] " (Author's coll.)

That is how the partial occupation of Vauquois did not even last more than an hour but engendered 799 dead, wounded and missing. In the valley, in Boureuilles, the 150th Brigade was totally pinned down on the ground as soon as they left the trenches and did not advance farther than 80 metres.

Despite a heavy toll for such meaningless results, Sarrail felt he almost succeeded and asked Joffre if he could renew the operation. The latter accepted and promised a fresh supply of ammunitions for 27th February. Sarrail ordered another assault for 28th February.

## In Vauquois

On 28th February, the 10th D.I started another attack against Vauquois. It was a failure once again. However, Micheler ordered to launch the attack again on the day after, whereas the troops were exhausted or lacking men and the ammunitions for the artillery were running short.

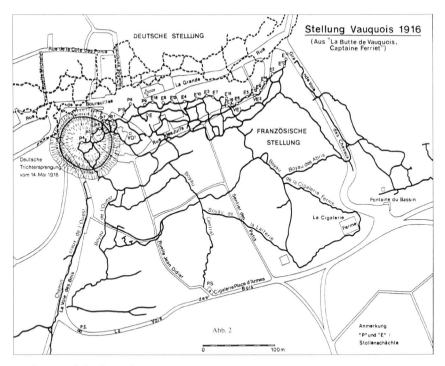

*A map of the French and German positions in Vauquois.*

On 1st March at 2 pm, the 31st R.I. left the trenches. No other men had come to relieve the troops since 17th February. Still, their bravery was wonderful. In half an hour, they overcame the whole German first line. At 6 pm, the French held the whole village except the area around the church where the remnants of four German regiments were still fighting. All the French assaults meant to defeat them were vain and at night, the 89th R.I. was pushed back. *" Our line of resistance is set up in the south of the main street of the village. The units are very mixed up and the death toll is significant, mostly for officers."*

Despite this horrifying night of fighting and the battles of the following days, the positions did not change anymore : the Germans held the hillock and the northern side of the village whereas the French held the southern part.

After several unsuccessful attempts above ground, both sides went on fighting under-

24

ground. The Butte de Vauquois gradually became a real underground stronghold that each side tried to blow up. Mines and camouflets followed each other until the total destruction of the village was completed. Not a single stone remained. On 14th May 1916, an incredibly powerful German mine blew up the west of the hillock, leaving a huge 32 meter- deep crater.

This senseless war did not allow to advance a single meter and the front uselessly remained stuck on the Butte de Vauquois until September 1918, even if the position had long lost all its strategic significance. The area of the Argonne had indeed entered a lethargic phase since the end of 1915.

*A view near the point X at the Éparges a little after its capture. The dead are removed from the trenches to clear the way. (Author's coll.)*

# André Pézard, the "Genevoix" of Vauquois

André Pézard, Second Lieutenant of the 46th R.I. spent most of the war on the Butte de Vauquois. He wrote a book of his war memories *"Nous autres à Vauquois"*, which remains one of the most heartrending book ever written on the First World War. This very book, first published in the Renaissance du Livre in 1919 is difficult to find today and has never been translated in English. One of the most striking passages takes place during the night fight on 1st March 1915, when the French finally arrived in the devastated village. Pézard has to lead his men to the front line but a small wall is on their way. Having to run without cover petrifies them. Pézard must insult them to urge them to advance :

" *You can see there's no danger. Go on! Move it! Bunch of fools, your fellows didn't die of it! And you "fourneau" will you get up? Don't make me kick your butt like a Boche! You are French soldiers, damn it! You belong to the 46th! Move on!*

*Two or three poor fellows hesitate for a second before jumping and have their heads blown up. They fall without a word and this slaughter scares the others.*

*All of a sudden, I find myself awful, harsh and cowardly at the same time. Although I am standing while the others remain lying against the awful scars of the ground, I take advantage of my rank and of the mute approval of my chiefs to insult these poor men who agreed to face a dreadful death. Disgusted, but knowing there are no other means, I keep throwing insults like a crazy man, two or three pieces of abuse, always the same ones, but more and more hateful; I offend poor men in the midst of all the dead.*"

At daybreak, in the conquered centre of the village, in front of the ruins of the church, the battle goes on :

*"Just give the charges to him!*

*A daredevil Poilu crawled on the heaps of stones in front of the church and the pale dawn shows us the man who quickly lights the explosives, throws them through the breach and then takes shelter between the rubble stones. And he did it again, briskly, violently, and carefully at the same time. But the Boches strike back.*

*Bang! A hideous column of tawny and black smoke bursts and spreads in the sky, hiding the ruins entirely.*

*Watch out! Another one!*

*These men are amazing. They are all on edge but keep yelling to one another that there is nothing to fear. And they keep up their position*".

# THE ÉPARGES

From September 1914 to April 1915, the French command kept trying to clear Verdun, on the west side in the Argonne and on the east side in Woëvre. In this area and on the Hauts-de-Meuse, French efforts were tremendous. The salient made by the Bavarians in September 1914 was a concern on many levels: first, it extended the French front line and thus kept a consequent amount of forces back. Secondly, it cut off the railroads from Verdun to Bar-le-Duc.

A quick glance at the map showed that the salient in Saint-Mihiel could be easily caught in a pincer movement in Woëvre plain, isolating thus the German positions on the Hauts-de-Meuse. The staff immediately noticed it and as soon as the battles calmed down in the North and in Belgium, Joffre prepared plans. However, to make a future offensive in the Woëvre easier, the French lacked look-out posts on the Hauts de

*Organization of the German stations conquered in the Éparges. The ground is utterly upside down after two months of uninterrupted battles, from February to April 1915. Maurice Genevoix, in Ceux de Quatorze, depicted with memorable skills the lives of soldiers sacrificed for the capture of the Éparges ridge. (Author's coll.)*

*Common grave down the Éparges ridge, maybe at the current location of the cemetery called du Trottoir, where victims of the attacks of February, March and April 1915 were buried, including Second Lieutenant Porchon, Maurice Genevoix's best friend. (Author's coll.)*

Meuse which would have allowed them to have a broader view of the plain and to aim artillery fires. One look-out post was however at arm's length, namely the Éparges ridge.

The first attack was planned for 17th February 1915. The objective of the 12th D.I. was the western side of the ridge, in order to set up a strong starting point for a full conquest. Like in Vauquois, the French would have to attack an amazingly well defended place from the valley. The initial assault by the artillery was to last one hour, with the last five minutes " at full speed". At the same time, several mines would be sent on the German front line.

On 17th February, everything happened according to the plan. Four mine explosions took place at 2 pm, and the infantry started an assault made difficult by the state of the terrain. But in the German trenches of the front line, only corpses were to be found. The victory was ultimate, even astonishingly easy for the French. The whole western side of the ridge was captured. Night protected the French from any German counter-attack. But on the day after, on

18th February, the enemy launched six strong assaults while the artillery crushed the newly conquered positions. In the following days, a ruthless battle started on the top of the Éparges. Lacking ammunitions, the French guns could not back up the foot soldiers. When the battle finally ended on 22nd February, the French still controlled the western stronghold and the Germans were masters of the eastern side of the ridge. The positions, gained thanks to terrible human sacrifices in the 12th Division, did not even offer a better view on Woëvre plain. On a purely strategic basis, the battle was useless.

## The assault on March 1915

Because of the poor results, General Herr, the head of the 1st Army, decided to launch other assaults in March 1915. For several weeks, substantial works were made to adjust the front lines in order to enable the infantry to safely reach its positions of departure. In the attack of the 18th March, the artillery backup was to be significant : fifteen field batteries, four pieces of 120 mm long-distance guns, two batteries of 120mm

*View of the German positions conquered on the Éparges ridge, in March 1915. The Germans will never be entirely chased away from the hill even if they lost the control of the top. On 27th March, the battle killed 700 French soldiers. As General Roques admitted it himself, the results were not worth all the casualties : "1° On the western salient, we set foot in a sixty meter-deep trench that we first occupied. 2° On the eastern salient, we came closer to the first line trench". From January to March 1915, the 1st Army lost, mainly on the front of the Éparges, 274 officers (84 dead) and 15,546 men (3,050 dead and 1,546 missing ). (Author's coll.)*

short-distance, two batteries of 155mm rapid fire. The goal was simple, namely to conquer the entire Éparges ridge.

Once again, the capture of the German first line took place quite easily but it was then impossible to advance. The assaults continued to be launched for three days, in vain. The battle ended with 1,300 casualties and a short 300 meter advance for the French army. General Herr clearly thought that the assaults had to be renewed as soon as possible.

On 27th March, the 12th DI launched a similar attack for the third time. It was another slaughter. 300 meters of German trenches were captured. As usual, the Germans counter-attacked at night and partly regained the ground which had been lost.

# The fiasco of the attack in the Woëvre

We previously explained the tactical and strategic significance of an offensive in Woëvre plain. At the beginning of 1915, Joffre sketched a plan: a surprise attack by two army corps in the North (the 1st and the 2nd) and by the 12th in the South. General Gérard was given the command of the northern detachment which was the biggest one. On the very eve of the attack, planned on 5th April, Gérard complained that he only had 196 pieces of 75 mm and a single battery of 155mm short distance rapid-fire guns.

It had been raining since 3rd April and Woëvre plain was a real swamp. Men would have to attack on a water-logged terrain. On the eve of the assault, Pichot-Duclos, an official of the General Headquarters, made a report which was utterly naïve. Consider for instance the following remark : " *We fear that today's artillery*

adjustments might be bothered by this misty weather."*

Actually, no adjustment could be made on that day and the men had to attack without artillery backup. Pichot-Duclos also wrote : "*We cannot use the artillery at night like in Champagne because it would be its last action. That is why the artillery will have to start from further back, on free ground, but this new way of attacking is not disapproved by General Guillaumat, on the contrary. To finish, the hour of the attack will depend on the weather: it will be launched as soon as the sky is clear, but we shall attack by tomorrow anyway.*"

To sum it up, the men would have to attack without cover on more than a kilometre, whatever the weather.

The result was, of course, dreadful, as Abel Ferry, a subaltern officer and Secretary of State, wrote it : "*The new artillery brought in this quagmire is impossible to adjust. Shells just*

*A 75mm gun during the attacks of 1915. During the attack in Woëvre, the French army had 196 75 mm guns, which was not enough to break through the German front. (Author's coll.)*

* Letter from Commandant PichotDuclos to the general comman- der-in-chief, 4th April, 1915.

31

*fizzle out in this mud. The breaches made by guns in the barbwire are useless or inexistent."*

When the infantry left its position around 1 pm, it was mown down under enemy fire. It was a failure everywhere and the toll was heavy. The attack was launched again a day after but it led to the same poor results. On 7th April, General Dubail suspended the general attack, at last. The battle of the Woëvre continued with skirmishes and precise fightings. This was the stage called limitation of the attack front. A final major attempt was made on the 12th in Marcheville. It was a thorough defeat.

The attack was suspended for good. Nobody gained any territory except for the Éparges where the 12th Division was sacrificed on the ridge for the fourth time. From 5 th - 9th April, the battle went on and claimed 5,000 French lives and probably as many on the German side. After an unparalleled slaughter, the French finally managed to reach point X, the last German stronghold on the ridge. 80% of the ridge remained controlled by the 12th D.I. Despite the mine warfare which would take place there until mid 1916, the front would no longer change position until September 1918. Nothing could better exemplify the uselessness of those battles of 1915 than the following remark from the Crown Prince :*"We wondered how the French nation could ever make up for such slaughters."*

Sure that the French would keep on sacrificing their troops to gain a few meters, the German command decided to accelerate the pace and strike Verdun.

# THE GERMAN ATTACK IN VERDUN

After the defeat of September 1914 in the Marne and the status quo in the race to the sea, Germany remained on the defensive in 1915, at least on the Western Front. At the beginning of 1916, it was believed that the German army would strike again on the West, on the French front, but nobody knew where. Intelligence coming from Germany was contradictory. General-in-Chief von Falkenhayn was surely hesitant himself. At the end of 1915, an attack against Belfort seemed to be bound to happen. It was planned for the end of January. But meanwhile, von Falkenhayn was convinced by the Crown Prince's chief of staff to attack Verdun. What were the arguments which urged him to favour Verdun for an attack? First of all, the Germans had learnt at the end of 1915 that all the forts of Verdun had just been disarmed. Secondly, the strategic position of Verdun was favourable for an attack. The fortified town was

*A camouflaged Krupp piece of heavy artillery on railway, ready for the offensive against Verdun. More than 1,000 guns were lined up in February 1916. Péricard wrote in his famous book about Verdun :*
*"There are 150 mm and Minenwerfer to destroy the walls, fill up the trenches and bury its defenders. There are 210 mm and 305 mm to pull down oak trees and beeches, to shatter clusters of trees. There are also 380 mm to smash concrete defence works [...] and 420 mm to pound forts". (IWM)*

*Burial of seven soldiers killed at the beginning of 1916. The Germans knew well the French presence in Verdun because of the raids which had allowed them to capture prisoners and above all thanks to a traitor who gave much intelligence to the Germans before the war was declared. They also knew about the disarming of the fortress which had started in 1915, which probably made them choose Verdun. (Author's coll.)*

threatened on both sides by the breakthroughs of September 1914 : in the South, the railroad to Bar-le-Duc was cut off in Saint-Mihiel. In the West, the German stations in Argonne allowed them to aim artillery fire toward the railroad in Châlons. Given that Verdun was isolated in the middle of the German front, it would not be easily supplied by the French. On 6th January 1916, Verdun was chosen as a major war objective.

## The German Preparations and the French lack of preparation

Since the attack against Verdun was to be the most tremendous one since August 1914, the preparations were really significant. Ten divisions were gathered on a reduced front:

VII. Reserve Korps : 13. R.D and 14. R. D.
XVIII. Armeekorps : 21. ID. and 25. ID.
III. Armeekorps : 5. ID. And 6. ID.
XV. Armeekorps : 30. I.D and 39. I.D.

V. Reserve-Korps which held the front with the 9. R.D. and 10. RD and which was to withdraw at the last minute to give way for the assault divisions.

In front of them, the French only had three divisions in line. The German supremacy was all the more obvious since the Crown Prince managed to line up 1,000 guns.

The lack of preparation on the French side was clearly illustrated by the poor conditions of the forts in Verdun. As the war was going on, the forts were gradually dismantled. The ammunitions and artillery shortages were so severe that they were directly taken from the forts as early as October 1914. On 9th August 1915, the fortified area of Verdun was created : forts were no longer autonomous and lost their own garrison in order to become resistance spots if under attack.

All the heavy pieces of artillery of Verdun's forts were requisitioned for the battle of Champagne in 1915. In October, 75 mm guns

*Two pictures of lookouts during Verdun's battle. The picture below was taken before the beginning of the attack. The trench is still well-organized with sandbags and barbwire. On the picture on top, the ground is utterly upside down and the periscope of the lookout is leaning against a shapeless wall. (IWM and author's coll.)*

*German preparation before the battle : tons of shells are brought by train to the front where big depots were built. The shells are protected in a three-part wicker basket.*
*(IWM)*

*Some idea of the amount of shells used during the battle.*
*(Ysec's coll.)*

were requisitioned as well. The retractable turret guns were the only ones which were not dismantled because they were impossible to remove. General Dubail even gave the order to blow up the forts in case of attack! However, one should not believe that the French were taken by surprise by the German attack.

At the end of January 1916, the G.H.Q believed that a massive attack was bound to happen, maybe in the North or against Paris, but more likely against Verdun. On 10th February, some reliable and minutely precise information arrived at the G.H.Q. The information said that the Crown Prince had been setting up for a few days now in the house of Henri Daverdier's widow, in Spincourt. The report started with this clear statement : *"The Germans are going to launch a large-scale attack against Verdun's area."* Measures were then taken to reinforce defences in the area and the defenders in Verdun were warned against an impending attack, but its importance was underestimated.

## The Assault

On 21st February 1916, at about 7.30 am, a thousand German guns started shelling the French lines. At the same time, six divisions were about to attack. On the French side, 12 battalions were on the first line and 24 in reserve. They were backed up by 131 pieces of field artillery (including 89 75 mm guns ) and 140 pieces of heavy artillery, including only 14 rapid-fire guns. Two divisions and a half were in reserve, ready to intervene quickly.

The German bombing aimed at the French first lines but also at the rear front and the artillery batteries were drowned under a rain of gas shells. Forts were also pounded by heavy artillery.

At 4 pm, the German infantry launched the assault. The French lines were totally thrown in confusion.

*A long 210-mm gun firing. The effects of Trommelfeuer were dreadful, as G. Champeaux, a liaison officer of the 164th R.I. stationed in Herbebois, described it :*
*" Trees are swept away as if they were feathers, smoke comes out of some shells, the dust formed by the ground turned upside down makes a fog which prevents us from seeing anything. We have to run out of our shelters and remain crouching in a large shell-hole. We are surrounded by corpses and wounded soldiers we cannot even help." (IWM)*

The German advance was not homogeneous. Around the Bois d'Haumont, the troops went quite fast. But in some other places, they were often confronted with isolated French groups who had survived the bombings and who fought without any connection with other units or with the rear front.

Even in Verdun, the French staffs did not know much about what was going on. A first message telling that the infantry was attacking only reached the 30th Army Corp at 4.45 pm : The 72th DI noticed an attack against the Bois d'Haumont. At 6.50 pm, a more precise account arrived : *"The first line in the Bois Des Caures seems to have been taken."* A little before midnight, the last report left no doubt about the situation : *" The Germans entirely control the Bois d'Haumont. A counter-attack will be prepared to take it back."*

At the same time, the French sent the 37th Division near the front line.

In the morning of 22nd February, the exhausted and disorganized units on the front lines were nevertheless ready to counter-attack.

38

But a little before 5 am, despite the falling snow and the darkness, the Germans started firing again with a rare violence. The remnants of trenches were crushed, French guns put out of order and counter-attacks suppressed before they could start. As early as 7.30 am, the German infantry renewed the assaults, sometimes with flamethrowers. In the afternoon, the Bois Des Caures was captured and Lieutenant Colonel Driant, a famous writer and a former deputy for Nancy, was killed alongside his chasseurs.

At 5 pm, the Germans took the ruins of Haumont. At the end of the day, they managed to reach the second French line almost everywhere. Threatened by the German advance, the artillery had to withdraw.

On that very day, German pressure caused the loss of the town of Brabant-sur-Meuse and the breakthrough of the second French line at the Wavrille.

On the 24th, the German advance fastened the pace, particularly in the east and west of the front. The second French line was cut off. The

*An old French 120 mm gun of Bange type, shattered by the German artillery. Captain Seguin of the 59th Batallion of Chasseurs on foot recounts :*
*"The violence of the shelling was such that when we went out of our shelters, we could not recognize the landscape we had been used to for four months. There was almost no standing tree left, it was difficult to move because of all the shell-holes which had turned the ground upside down. Secondary defences were seriously damaged, but there was such a tangle of trees and barbwire that the place still remained a serious obstacle for the enemy". (Author's coll.)*

39

*On the left, next to his brothers who also had their arm hurt, Lieutenant von Brandis is posing for posterity. This uncommon photograph allows us to know the face of this famous man.*

situation became really worrying but reinforcements started arriving in Verdun. At the end of the day, the Germans were only ten kilometres away from the town. On the front line, the situation was really confused.

# THE TRUTH ABOUT THE CAPTURE
# OF FORT DOUAUMONT

After the war, General Passaga translated into French the account of Lieutenant von Brandis about the capture of Fort Douaumont. The modesty of the officer guarantees the truthfulness of the following words :

"[…] *Lieutenant Brandis shouts to his men : "To Douaumont". But they think their officer has gone crazy. The company hesitates when a fellow stands up and yells "There'll be beds over there!" He is immediately followed by the officers and the bravest soldiers. The small group arrives at the barbwire networks above the ditch of the fort. They cut them off with a pair of pliers. Being ensured by patrols that the counterscarp coffres are empty of defenders, the small band sneaks into the ditch thanks to poles. Then, they climb over the fort, under the snow, and arrive in the yard, the blockhouse doors are open. They enter the blockhouse and run into a few dozen unarmed and dumbfounded men.*

*A couple of minutes later, Captain Haupt, who commanded the company who was close to that of Brandis, entered the fort, following Brandis. Then, the Germans counted the men: they were 98, including 19 officers. It was not enough to defend a huge fort like Douaumont.*

*Brandis had to go back to get reinforcements, food and ammunitions. At night, with a few men, as he was making his way through the snow thanks to a compass, he ran into men of his company and of Haupt's. They were about 300 hiding in shell-holes. Following Brandis's orders, ensured that the way was clear and that they would find " food, beds and stoves", these men decided to go, at last".*

.

## The capture of Fort Douaumont

25th February was really a hard day for French defences, even if on the day before, the Germans had thought they had broken through the front and had made their way to Verdun. On the 25th , Fort Douaumont was captured by the Germans without a fight. It was partly due to a major mistake by the French command. Indeed,

17 - La Bataille de Verdun. - Le Ravin de la Dame, surnommé le Ravin de la Mort
A droite de la Route, le Bois du Chauffour; à gauche, le Bois de Navvé
The Battle of Verdun - The hollow way of the « Dame » surnamed « Hollow way of the death »
On the right of the way, the wood of Chauffour, on the left, the wood of Navvé

*Two views of the Ravin de La Dame, called the Ravin de la Mort (ravine of death) at two different times. On top, the picture was taken a few months after the end of the war. Below, it was taken in 1916. In both cases, the landscape is lunar, all the more since there used to be the Bois de Chauffour on the right and the Bois de Nawé on the left of the road. (Ysec's coll.)*

*On the right page, a French defender in an unidentified fort of Verdun. (IWM)*

after a four-day battle, nobody ordered to occupy Fort Douaumont. Whereas the Germans were coming closer, they were only 57 artillerymen, mostly territorial and thus older soldiers, to man the few guns which were still working in the fort. The old NCO who commanded them, Battery Guardian Chenot, decided to aim at already defined distant targets. But he was far from imagining the Germans were so close.

Moreover, the officers who commanded the men who fought around the fort had absolutely

no idea that this one was almost empty. Thus, they fought as if the fort was not there, sure that the garrison was ready to defend it.

In the mid-afternoon of 25th February, Oberleutnant Brandis, at the head of the 8th Company of the 24 I.R. from Brandebourg, arrived close to the fort. The building was impressive but seemed astonishingly still. Brandis decided to go and see by himself, followed by a small band of soldiers from the same unit, under the orders of Hauptmann Haupt. Without even realizing it, they had captured the fort without a fight.

## The 2nd Army gets ready

When Fort Douamont was captured by the Germans, General Joffre met General Pétain in his HQ in Chantilly and gave him the command of the area of Verdun. At that time, Pétain was head of the 2nd Army but had only his staff with him. From then on, all the troops fighting in Verdun or heading for the front were systematically sent under the command of Pétain, in the 2nd Army, whose HQ set up in Souilly, twenty kilometres away from the fortress. That meant

*General Pétain became renowned through the offensive in Artois in April 1915. He was urgently called in to Chantilly by General Joffre to get the command of the area of Verdun. A brilliant coordinator and a charismatic leader, General Pétain revealed his skills during the war in which he started as a colonel. His career was moving slowly in peace time because of his controversial opinions but it definitely soared during the war. He was promoted General de Brigade before the end of 1914, commanded an army corps at the beginning of 1915, became a general at the start of the battle of Verdun. During summer 1916, he was given the command of a group of armies and became General-in-chief of the French armies in May 1917. (IWM)*

*Two views of a 15 cm gun firing during Verdun's battle. Péricard described very vividly, at the beginning of his book, the poor fate of men who were going through bombings :*
*"deafened by the noise, dizzy with smoke, suffocating with gas, they are thrown against the ground or hurled against each other in the blasts. Pieces of shrapnel whistle in their ears. The soil, the stones, the riffles, the beams of the shelters and the equipment all spring out and then fall down around them. Sometimes, something warm sticks to their cheek and it's a piece of brain [...] ". (IWM)*

that Pétain would be able to coordinate alone the defence of Verdun, and thus be more efficient.

Pétain arrived in Souilly on 25th February at 11pm. He started commanding an hour later. He was, as he later wrote with humour : " *already responsible for everything, without any means of action yet.*"

On 26th February, the French were busy trying to capture Fort Douaumont. There was only time for a single attempt before the launching of another German offensive : the 2nd Battalion of the 1st Mixed Regiment advanced

to the barbwire fence of the fort, without besieging it. Around noon, the Germans rushed onwards from the whole length of the front. They captured an annex of the fort, the fortifications of Hardaumont. In the western area, a slope called Côte du Poivre was also captured. The bombing was so violent that on the eastern part of the front, the 44th Territorial was forced to leave Fort Vaux. But it was reinvested before the Germans could ever control it.

That episode exemplifies the whole day of 26th February. After a promising start, it ended up very badly for the Germans who were held in check everywhere. For the first time, a gleam of hope appeared for the French side and Pétain obtained a little respite. Indeed, the Germans used so many ammunitions during those days of battle that they had to wait for the supply. The intensity of the battle decreased for a couple of days.

*French artillerymen unlimbering a 65 mm moutain gun in a very low ceilinged- casemate. Colonel Thomasson depicted the state of French artillery at the beginning of the battle in the following manner :*
*"As we lacked equipment, like logs for instance, the shelters built by the batteries were sure to collapse on our heads with the first serious bombardment; a lot of them were not even field explosive-proof".*
*(IWM)*

# THE FRENCH GET ORGANIZED

*It was too often written that the French army only had the chests of the Poilus to fight against the German material superiority. That is absolutely wrong and even if the artillery is less numerous on the French side, equipment is not lacking as we can see it with the amazing organization of the "Voie Sacrée" (Holy Road ). On this road which linked Bar-le-Duc to Verdun, lorries follow one another every 16 seconds during the whole duration of the battle! 3,500 lorries are in charge of supplying the 2nd Army. They carry an average of 90,000 men and 50,000 tons of equipment per week.*
*(IWM)*

## Pétain set up in Souilly

As soon as he arrived in Souilly, Pétain organized the front. Once the surprise was over, it was time to rationalize defence. The first general order of operations planned the mission of the 2nd Army (to defend Verdun at any cost) and its composition. The army was divided into four groups, that is to say eleven divisions (then twelve). The most dangerous sector was put

*The City hall in Souilly where General Pétain set up. (Ysec's coll.)*

under the supervision of Guillaumat and Balfourier's groups, from the Meuse to Eix.

Pétain also cancelled the order to destroy forts which had been given by General Herr. He also limited the withdrawal from the Woëvre area, in order to prevent the Germans from setting up their artillery there and aim at Verdun.

To finish, he also organized the traffic on the road from Bar-le-Duc to Verdun, which would soon be known as the "Voie Sacrée", the only secure way to reach the front.

On 27th February, the German bombing of the French front lines raged on but all the infantry assaults launched at the end of the day failed. It was the same on the day after. The German advance came to a standstill. A French counter-attack launched on Fort Douaumont was abandoned because of the German pressure : on 2nd March, the men of the Crown Prince took the village of Douaumont, lost it on the day after, and then set up there for good on 4th March.

*Two views of the Voie Sacrée which is divided into sections, like the railroad, in order to avoid traffic jam or accidents. Thousands of roadmen keep repairing the road on a daily basis and any broken down vehicle is thrown onto the side of the road.*
*(IWM and author's coll.)*

*The German heavy gun at Sorel Farm, shooting at a distant target on the area of Verdun. Colonel Thomasson wrote : "The infantry was the martyr, not the queen of the battles from 21st to 25th February. The queen was the artillery. Contrary to opinions before the war, its role was tremendous because not only did it fire on front lines but, thanks to a frightful amount of ammunitions, it poured on deep positions and caused them to be untenable". (JL Kaluzko's coll.)*

## An attack on the left bank?

The German advance on the right bank of the Meuse river was a couple of kilometres farther than the French positions on the left bank, on the Mort-Homme hill for instance. That situation was worrying because the German artillerymen soon aimed their guns at the West, which allowed them to rake most positions of Bazelaire's group. From 29th February onwards, the bombing was ceaseless. But the Germans were soon caught in their own trap. On 29th February, Pétain ordered the artillery of the 29th Division to be more aggressive. It was soon the entire artillery of the left bank which raked the newly conquered German positions. Taken sideways by the fire of the 75mm, the movements of the German troops were made very difficult. Any advance of the Crown Prince's men was immediately stopped in the area which bordered the Meuse. This situation impelled the Germans to take the battle on the left bank.

On the eve of another German attack, French organizations were very poor. In some cases, defence works were not even finished, in others, bombings had caused significant damage:

*"All the 2nd position and the rear zone of batteries look like a skimmer, with holes everywhere. Our entanglements on the opposite-slope, behind the ridge of the Côte du Mort-Homme and the Côte de l'Oie, are torn into pieces and immediately repaired. Communication links are cut off (and re-established under the bombing) once per hour on average."*

On 6th March, the intensity of bombardment doubled and the German infantry went out of its trenches, encircled the village of Forges and then Regnéville. Some thick fog and swirling snow prevented the French from correctly observing the enemy advance. At night, the Germans took Forges and Regnéville with their defenders and arrived at the bottom of the Mort-Homme ridge.

On 7th March, the 11. and 12. R.D. of the 6th German Reserve Corp kept on with their assaults. The battle raged on in Cumièges

*German soldiers waiting for food supply in front of a field kitchen, a Goulaschkanone, as they were called. The steel helmet appeared during the battle of Verdun, but it is difficult though to give a precise date for its first use on the front line, since all the units did not get it at the same time.*
*(IWM)*

which was successively taken by both armies. The Bois des Corbeaux and Bois de Cumières were taken by the Germans and the 67th Division only managed to contain them thanks to all its reserve troops.

On 8th March, the French partly regained the grounds which had been lost on the day before. On 9th March, German progress was really limited, probably due to a lack of ammunitions. But on the 10th, the shelling started again and the battle intensified. After the loss of the Bois des Corbeaux and Bois de Cumières, the French counter-attacked on 11th March thanks to the backup of the 40th Division. They were stopped everywhere by German artillery. Some respite was then possible on the left bank of the Meuse river.

## Objective: Vaux

While the battle was raging on at Mort-Homme, the Germans kept on fighting on the eastern part of the battlefield, away from French sideway fires. The war objective of the enemy was Fort Vaux. On 8th March, a severe bombing struck that area, with teargas shells for instance. The village of Vaux was partly captured in the afternoon.

A German release dated from 9th March, 2 pm, victoriously claimed the capture of the village and Fort Vaux. A mistake made by German officers originated this false telegram. It surely caused some disillusionment in Germany when the public opinion was later told that the fort still belonged to the French.

On 10th March, the Germans renewed their assaults against the fort with multiplied strength. Several successive waves were stopped by 75's shells which caused a real inferno for the assailants. From 10th March 1916 onwards, the battle changed nature : on both banks of the Meuse river, the Germans started suffering as much as the French, sometimes even more.

Nevertheless, the threat on Fort Vaux remained serious. Pétain took a decision which went against the policy about forts which had been implemented since the outbreak of the war. From 12th March onwards, forts would no longer depend on infantry units on a practical level. On the contrary, each fort would obey its own com-

*A view of the pond of Vaux at the end of the war. If the story of Fort Vaux became famous, one should not forget that the whole area around the village and the pond was the scene of a particularly ruthless battle which lasted for several long weeks.*
*(Ysec's coll.)*

*Some German prisoners waiting to be evacuated. Here are three anecdotes told by Poilus in Verdun about these prisoners :*
*" The prisoners tell us : we shall not defeat you but you shall not either". (Leclaire)*
*" Our prisoner made it clear that he was glad to be a prisoner, that for him the war was over and that if he had hesitated so much before surrendering, it was because he had been told that the French killed all the prisoners with a bayo-net". (Suteau, 90th R.I.)*
*"One night, as we brought a prisoner, our sergeant put his gun against his head just to scare him; our Boche was not frightened at all and told him in perfect french : You can kill me, it will not prevent us from being victorious and reach Paris". (Officer Cadet Gourc, 142nd R.I).*
*(Ysec's coll.)*

mand and would be manned by its own garrison, in order to fight without the infantry and be able to resist even if besieged.

Reinforcement kept arriving and the 2nd Army counted twenty-three divisions and a half on 13th March. As for the enemy, the Crown Prince did not line up more than twenty-one of them. The Germans were thus slightly outnumbered by the French and that allowed Pétain to phone his subordinates the following message : *"Be brave, my friends, let's gather our strengths, the victory is in sight."*

## Hill 304

On 20th March 1916, German artillery suddenly triggered assaults against Hill 304 with a fury which had not been seen since 21st February. A massive assault was brooding. At 3.10 pm, an alarming report from the balloon of the 36th Compagnie d'Aérostiers read: *"Amazingly violent bombings above the trenches in the Bois de Malancourt. Three huge blasts with burst of flames rising at least 100 metres above ground have just taken place."* Twenty minutes later, another incoming message from the balloon said: *"The three huge black clouds first reported were not caused by blasts but by attacks with inflamed liquid."* The flame-thrower attack was later confirmed by *"tongues of fire"* seen on the Avocourt-Malancourt road.

After the bombing, the defenders were on their knees. Huge jets of inflamed liquid terrorized the survivors in such a way that twenty companies, or rather what remained of them, were made prisoners by the Bavarians of the 11. I.D.

On 8th April, a new German breakthrough caused the defenders in Béthincourt to be in dire straits. On 9th April, the Germans were ready to renew the assault on the left bank with a tremendous amount of ammunitions, as usual. At noon, the infantry started attacking against Mort-Homme and Hill 304 at the same time. The French line yielded ground but did not give in. That was the reason for Pétain's optimism in his 10th April order :

*German soldiers carrying guns on their shoulder. All of them wear a steel helmet with an escutcheon on it, which was quite rare during WW1. The meaning of it is not known but it may be the emblem of a unit. (IWM)*

*"9th April was a glorious day. All the furious assaults of the Crown Prince's soldiers were crushed everywhere. Foot soldiers, artillerymen, sappers, aviators of the 2nd Army behaved like heroes, let us honour them all. The Germans shall attack again, may each one of you work and remain watchful to be as successful as the day before. Be Brave, we shall get them."*

The most important event of this end of April was Pétain being replaced by Nivelle at the head of the 2nd Army. Pétain was indeed appointed commander of the group of armies of the Centre. He thus commanded the 2nd, 3rd, 4th and 5th Armies. That promotion was only a step since a year later, after the tragic episode of the Chemin des Dames, Pétain will be appointed at the highest rank, that is to say général en chef, commander in chief of the French armies.

When Pétain was replaced by Nivelle at the head of the 2nd Army, the battle was far from being over. However, the Germans were far from the victory. Although the French had lost 3,000 officers and 130,000 men (killed, wounded, missing) the front had not been disrupted and the situation was stabilized. Forty divisions fought in Verdun but the French army had not lost all its strengths. Joffre was even able to keep forty divisions for the offensive in the Somme. On the German side, anxiety prevailed, as the following remark from the Crown Prince illustrates it : "*I doubted more and more everyday that the French, who used a quick relief system, should suffer more losses than we did.*"

*Supply chores in the Fleury area. The good state of the buildings tends to prove that the picture was taken before the outbreak of the battle of February 1916. An anonymous Poilu, probably an officer, wrote : " It seems the high command did not pay as much attention to food supplies as they did to the ammunition supply. Couldn't they have thought about better food for the men on the front than boiled rice which turns sour in a couple of hours? Should they have taken the time to taste the beans, they might have wondered why those beans always smelled like wet dog." (Author's coll.)*

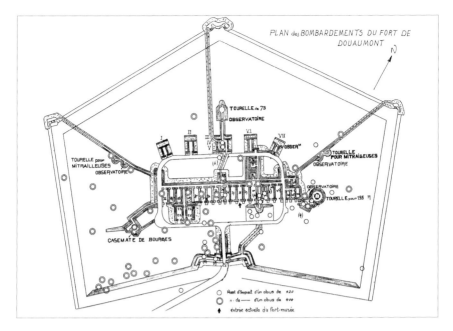

*A plan of the bombing of Fort Douaumont. (Ysec's coll.)*

# BATTLES FOR THE FORTS

As soon as he was at the head of the 2nd Army, Nivelle prepared the recapture of Fort Douaumont. However, he critically lacked men. Since the front was stabilized in Verdun, Joffre was entirely devoted to the offensive in the Somme. As a result, Nivelle was only given a single division, the 5th D.I. of General Mangin, for a one kilometre-long front. Another division would be available in reserve though.

It was all the more scarce since the Germans did not remain idle. On the left bank of the Meuse river, they managed to capture the most important part of Hill 304, which offered them a direct view on Mort-Homme. Whereas the French were about to attack Fort Douamont, the Germans struck heavily in Mort-Homme on 20th May.

*A portrait of General Mangin whose career had its ups and downs during the war, including a dismissal after the failure of April 1917.*
*(Ysec's coll. )*

*The capture of Fort Douaumont, on 25th February 1916, did not trigger the collapse of the French front in the area and the battle went on for weeks in order to capture surrounding sectors, like Thiaumont works for instance. The FT-3 pillbox "abri de combat FT-3", near Thiaumont. From May to September 1916, the struggle was particularly fierce there. (Ysec's coll.)*

Attacks kept raging on until 23rd May when the top of the hill remained German. On the day after, the village of Cumières was captured as well. The situation was getting critical since the Germans were in control of both hills of the left bank. They were thus able to aim at French artillery which was such a hindrance to their advance on the right bank. Tactically speaking, that success was a tremendously significant one for the Crown Prince.

## The assault on Fort Douaumont

While the attack was turning into a French failure on the left bank, Nivelle and Mangin were preparing the offensive against Fort Douaumont. The initial assaults of artillery were particularly important since they lasted for five days, during which all the targets and their surroundings received a thousand tons of shells per day! That was meant to ruin the defences as much as the morale of the enemy.

Moreover, given the narrowness of the attack front, Mangin launched a series of limited attacks meant to ensure security on the flanks of the assault. Except for a few ones,

I
W
M

they all failed. Consequently, the first conditions which had to be fulfilled before attacking were not fulfilled. But the order to attack was given anyway. On 22nd May, at 11.50 am, the French infantry walked out of the trenches and rushed on. Ten minutes later, the battalion of the 129th R. I. positioned on the right, had reached the superstructures of the fort. While the 129th R.I. managed to reach the fort, the 74th was stopped a few metres away from the other one. On both flanks, the advance was very small. At the same time, the battle was raging on in the sky. The French air force set fire to six out of eight Drachens (captive balloons) which were aiming the fire of the German artillery.

On the fort itself, the battles were tremendously ruthless.

*A band of defenders of the Côte du Poivre, in May 1916. Soldier Branchen of the 405th recounts : "The relief, at last. In this elite regiment where two weeks ago you could find ten volunteers when one was needed, courage was getting thin on the ground. As we go out of the barracks of Bevaux, we come across a regiment heading for the front. These men look at us with fear in the eyes and ask us :*
*Which company are you in the 405th?*
*We are the regiment!"*

*A French piece of 155 mm at the bottom of the Côte de Belleville, ready to shoot at the plateau of Douaumont. By 1st June 1916, the artillery of the 2nd Army counted : 1,777 guns, including 1,184 field artillery pieces (1,073 pieces of 75mm, 8 pieces of 65mm mountain guns, 26 pieces of 80mm and 77 pieces of 90mm ), 174 short-distance pieces of heavy artillery, 400 long-distance pieces of heavy artillery and 19 high-powered pieces of artillery. (IWM)*

The assailants only held the south-western part of the superstructure. In the fort itself, the Germans did not suffer much and they violently fired from the casemates and the turrets.

At sunset, the situation had not changed much. A single battalion of the 129th R.I. had maintained its advanced position, utterly isolated, on the top of the fort.

On 23rd May at 9 am, the Germans started to violently shell the French lines and the fort itself, its defenders being protected under a strong and heavy armour. The toll was heavy among the French ranks even if the retort of the artillery made any German counter-attack impossible. Relieving the fort quickly turned out to be impossible considering the strength of the defence. At the end of the day, General Mangin ordered the relief of the exhausted 5th D.I. by the 36th D.I. But it was actually too late to rescue the isolated soldiers on the top of the fort.

On 24th May, the Germans renewed their pounding and attacked with the infantry. That was the beginning of the end. The first attempt to

relieve Fort Douaumont ended up in a major defeat. As early as 25th May, the Germans regained and occupied their initial front line. Taking advantage of the chaos that prevailed among French ranks, the Germans even launched an attack in the Bois de Nawé which allowed them to break into the corner of the main defence line of Nivelle.

That second half of May was really nerve-racking for the French. The losses were significant since two exhausted battalions on the left bank and three on the right bank of the Meuse river had to be relieved. Moreover, the Germans had conquered several valuable strategic places that would be determining for future operations.

## Fort Vaux under siege

In the Somme, the Allies were going through with their preparations and the Germans knew an impending attack was bound to happen. They had to be victorious in Verdun before the outbreak of a French-British attack.

*Wounded soldiers from the battles of Vaux, waiting to be evacuated at Fort Tavannes. Soldier Baudoin from the 163th R.I. accurately portrayed a Poilu in Verdun :*
*"His face is gaunt, dirty, exhausted, darkened by gunpowder, he is covered with mud, his coat is torn off by barb wire. The Poilus who come back from that hell are but shadows, poor shadows who have just made boundless efforts [...] The Poilu is the new hero: humble, ignored, dirty, covered in lice, he has not washed or changed clothes in 15 days and he looked death in the face every single second for those 15 days".*
*(Ysec's coll.)*

*A view inside Fort Vaux, probably when it was relieved in November 1916. Despite ceaseless shelling with all kinds of calibres, the vaults resisted, thus proving the solidity of modernised Séré de Rivières forts. Like Fort Douaumont, Fort Vaux was a piece of masonry made of 1 to 1,5 m thick limestone rubble stones, reinforced by a 2,5 m thick layer of concrete, with a 1 m thick layer of sand between the two. The fort was thus invulnerable to 150, 210 and even 280 mm. (IWM)*

On 1st June, the enemy artillery started bombing the right flank of the first French line, more precisely on the Bois de la Caillette and Fort Vaux. Then, the infantry attacked, encircling all the defences in the wood and reaching the fortifications of the fort. French counter-attacks failed and the siege of the fort could start. The village of Damloup fell on 2nd June.

Official history relates : "*In Fort Vaux, the enemy took the north-east and north-west coffres. The fight went on in the galleries. The garrison (two companies of the 142th R.I and specialists : artillerymen, sappers, telegraphers), who was under the command of Raynal, found itself hindered rather than reinforced by all the isolated men who fled back into the fort.*"

In the evening of 2nd June, the Germans reached the top of the fort where they immediately put machine-guns which prevented any reinforcement from entering the fort. The garrison kept on fighting but the situation was becoming more than difficult.

*The shell of modernised forts resisted German fire except against the heaviest pieces like the 380 and 420 mm guns.*
*However, armoured domes and turrets were more vulnerable as this after-war postcard shows it. (Ysec's coll.)*

For Nivelle as well as General Lebrun who commanded the 3rd C. A. in the area, the prospect of losing the fort was dreadful and it had to be impelled at all costs.

During the night between 2nd and 3rd June, counter-attacks followed each other but none reached the fort. They were all swept away by the German artillery fire and machine-guns. At 5.50 am, on 3rd June, General Lebrun took the phone and called the head of the 124th D.I. : "*The fort must be immediately relieved at all costs and, since we have comrades there, with an attack led by the general of the D.I. himself if need be. Ask us anything you need and we shall give you satisfaction as much as we can.*" The situation had to be critical to ask a major general to lead his troops on the first line himself! An attack was launched the following night after strong initial assaults by the artillery but it did not reach the fort.

On 5th June, several visual messages coming from Vaux were received in Fort Souville. They were more and more insistent :

*View of the Vaux river at the apex of the battle in summer 1916. Everything was devastated by the artillery. The two German soldiers look disillusioned amidst this horrific landscape. The situation around Vaux was terrible for the French soldiers too, as Captain Delvert described it from his entrenchment R1 : "In our trenches, it is a tragedy : every where, stones are spotted with red drops; in the saps, stiff corpses are lying in their tent sheets which are covered with blood; there are heaps of unnameable remains everywhere". (IWM)*

" *7.55am : Where are you? No answer. Artillery, aim at central part of fort.*

*8.15 am : Can't hear your artillery. Are in the most dire plight. Immediate attack or we are lost.*

*8.20 am : Are attacked by gas and inflamed liquid. Can't hear artillery. In the most dire plight.*

*11. 05 pm : Day before…, I must be relieved tonight and water supply must arrive right now. I feel my strengths are leaving me. The troop, men and officers, did their duty all along and under all circumstances.*"

At 11.20 pm, Fort Souville received snatches of a desperate message :" *(…) 53…wounded…. aspire… losses… You will arrive before complete exhaustion. Vive la France!* "

In Souville, they could only answer the following words : "*Message received. Be brave.*"

The French command sent fresh troops on the front line who attacked on 6th June at 2 am. Despite the darkness, German machine guns, placed on the top of the fort, beat back the assault.

At 6.30 am, a longer message was received from Fort Vaux : *"I don't have anymore water although I've rationed it for the past few days, I need to be relieved and be supplied in water immediately. I feel I am losing all my strengths [...] Hope you will attack strongly again before total exhaustion."*

Consequently, Nivelle created a brigade with men from the left bank and planned an attack for 8th June.

But on 7th June at 3.30 am, a final message impossible to understand was received in Souville :

" ...hold on...". That was the end. A few hours later, a German release announced the fall of Fort Vaux. Suffering from thirst, the garrison had

*The quotation of Fort Vaux's last carrier pigeon. (Ysec's coll.)*

*Joffre rewards soldier Jouy, a hero of Vaux. (IWM)*

*The French artillery was ill-equipped, even during summer 1916, with out-dated equipment, namely slow-fire guns like Bange system ones. We can see them on this picture of an artillery depot taken on 14th June 1916. (IWM)*

to surrender but quite exceptionally, the Germans paid military honours to them.

On the French side, Nivelle refused to believe the German release and maintained the counter-attack planned on 8th June with the 2nd Zouave Regiment and the Moroccan Colonial Regiment. The Zouaves were mowed down by some very violent artillery fire before they managed to

*View of Fort Vaux on 22nd November 1916 after it was relieved. The concrete layer crumbles everywhere but was not broken through. The surroundings though are in a dreadful plight. (Author's coll.)*

reach their line of departure. The Moroccans advanced to the counterscarp of the fort where they were swept away by German machine-guns, as they had already been five times before.

On the same day, the Germans attacked by the West and took over Thiaumont works for a couple of hours. It was located on Fleury ridge and represented the last resistance line before Verdun. The battle went on in this area, with a relative decrease of intensity though, till mid-June.

## A final effort before the allied offensive

Around 20th June, the Crown Prince had ful-filled all the conditions to trigger an ultimate and successful offensive against Verdun. Indeed, with the fall of Fort Vaux, the eastern flank was tightly held. In the West, the capture of Mort-

*Tavannes Tunnel was described by Lieutenant Benech, 321th R.I., in the following words :*
*" 6th June 1916. We are arriving at the tunnel. Shall we be condemned to live here? […] Above us, under the vault, some dirty electric lamps cast a gloomy light and flies fly around in circle above our heads. Numb and annoying, they attack our skins […] At some places, something flows down the ground! Is it water or urine? There is an animal reek, a mix of excrement and corpse, sweat and human filth that makes you choke".*
*(Author's coll.)*

65

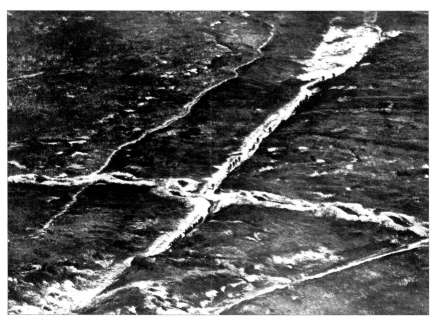

*A German attack on Verdun. We can see soldiers walking in single file in a shallow trench. During the offensive against Fleury on 11th July, the 217th R.I. was beaten back. Sergeant Bonfils recounts : "We fire all the more strongly since we know the danger is important. It is the strength born of despair which drives us all. But we are not numerous enough. During the night of relief, ten men were killed out of the 35 men of my half-section. The bombardments made other victims since then" .*
*(IWM)*

Homme prevented the French artillery from hindering German movements in the central area where a decisive breakthrough was about to be attempted.

On 21st June, a first massive attack fell on the French lines. From the evening of 22nd June onwards, the German artillery intensified and utterly drowned the French lines with poison gas, which remained in the bottom of ravines and considerably hindered the relief of troops. On both flanks, the German advance made no progress as opposed to the centre where they broke through the front, causing a very dangerous breach between two French army corps. In the surroundings of Souville, the 130th D.I. split into two parts. As early as 9 am, the village of Fleury was captured.

In the West, the right flank of the 129th D.I. was overwhelmed, the Germans advanced on the Côte de Froideterre, reached the shelter called Quatre Cheminées and Froideterre works which were encircled for a while.

If the Germans kept on advancing that fast, they would reach the heights above Verdun in a few hours. The situation had never been that critical since the first days of offensive in February.

All day long, the French kept counter-attacking, without gaining much lost grounds but it stopped the German advance. The junction between the 120th and the 130th remained very fragile. A counter-attack devised by Nivelle and launched on the 27th , renewed on the 28th and the 30th June, failed every time. The situation was a little better for the Germans who were technically able to capture Verdun. However, they had made no progress since 23rd June. Above all, the allied offensive in the Somme had just started. In order to maintain the front in that area, would the Germans be obliged to slow down in Verdun?

*Fighting units set up in areas which were rather little exposed, even though in Verdun, soldiers were exposed everywhere. Priest Fontan, a chaplain of the 96th R.I. wrote about the fact that there was not any safe shelter : "The Ravin du Gravier, at the point where the Ravin des Vignes ended, was the place for the food supply of the 96th . All of a sudden, a terrible bombing fell on the ravine, killing and wounding men, making survivors flee. Stretcher-bearer P. stood still, all alone. He used to be a doorman in Béziers and he knew how respectfully you had to treat good French wine. And the cask of wine was wounded and was losing all its blood through a large breach. P. first put his mouth against the hole and started drinking up all the content. It took quite a long time. Then, he took some bottles which were lying around and filled 25 of them. He brought them all to his squad. France has lost, he sombrely said to his comrades; the Poilus left the booze ! " (Author's coll.)*

# HOW THE GERMANS LOST
# THE BATTLE OF VERDUN

*Two German corpses
on the battlefield of
Fleury. On 11th July,
the battle was extremely
ruthless. The 217th R.I.
lost 33 officers and
1,300 men. On the front
of the 4th Battalion of
the 358th R.I. , the
defenders counted 400
German corpses.
(Author's coll.)*

At the beginning of July, the French defences
got organized around Fort Souville. It represented the last obstacle before reaching Verdun
and the Germans tried to break through it on
11th July. There was no time to lose because the
pressure of the allies in the Somme was tremendous.

From 9th July onwards, the German artillery
crushed the French lines. On the 11th, the
infantry attacked. It was contained in most areas

except for the Ravin de La Poudrière where two battalions were destroyed. The Bois de Fleury was reached and the central part of the front was broken through.

On the battlefield, General Mangin was in charge of the operations. He decided to counter-attack immediately. The assault was launched in the evening and turned out to be a total failure. Both battalions lost their way and did not even reach their starting position.

The operation would have to be renewed on the day after. But the Germans did not allow it since they launched their offensive at dawn. As violent as in the former assault, they tried to upset the French lines and managed to capture Sainte-Fine chapel and walk on Fort Souville.

At 9.20 am, the staff of Mangin's group got in touch with Lieutenant Champigny, 8th D.I. What they learnt was dreadful : " *At 8.55 am, artillery observatory reports that the Germans occupy Fort Souville, information confirmed by the observatory of the A.D 8 which reports a fight with grenades inside the fort.*"

*The ruins of Fort Souville right after the end of the war. Last important fort before Verdun, it was constantly bombed from 11th July onwards. Lieutenant Dupuy, who found shelter in it in the morning of 11th July, sent the following message to his superior, Colonel Borius, 7th R.I. : "After going through several barrages and clouds of poison gas, we painfully reached Fort Souville. There, everything is upside down. The commandant of the fort is intoxicated. The garrison is out of action. If not told otherwise, I shall stay in the fort and be in charge of the defence".*
*(Author's coll.)*

69

*The Voie Sacrée made possible the ammunition supply for the French artillery in Verdun. In July 1916, the number of guns available on the front of the 2nd Army decreased because of the battle in the Somme which required a lot of equipment. Joffre hoped indeed for a decisive breakthrough which will never take place. (Ysec's coll.)*

*German prisoners evacuated toward the rear front. The defeat of the 5. Armee in front of Fleury sounded the knell of German hopes of victory in Verdun. We can thus declare that in the evening of 12th July, the Germans definitely lost the battle of Verdun. (Author's coll.)*

The French had to recapture the fort or the front would be broken through. The Germans had never been so close to victory. But the French reaction was particularly fierce. The fort in itself had not surrendered and its defenders fought on the superstructures where they chased away the few German troops who had set up there. Several concentric counter-attacks were launched on the troops positioned at the extreme end of the German advance, and the artillery intensified at the same time.

On 12th July in the evening, Verdun was saved. The Crown Prince was given some very precise orders : " *Since the objectives could not be reache*d", he had to remain on "*a strictly defensive position*".

The French defence in Verdun and a huge pressure from the Allies in the Somme put an end to German hopes of victory. But the army of the Crown Prince was ready to sacrifice everything to keep the grounds which had been gained.

# THE RECAPTURE OF THE FORTS

During the summer, both French and German efforts were concentrated in the Somme where a very deadly battle was raging on. However, calm was not back in Verdun. During August, fighting took place around Fleury which was captured and lost several times just like Thiaumont. Both sides were fighting without any reserve troops and exhausted themselves for few results.

In September, the French kept on with precisely defined actions which allowed them to recapture Fort Souville, Fleury and to get closer to Fort Douaumont. Calm came back from 21st September onwards. This sort of truce enabled the French to prepare a massive attack against Douaumont.

On 3rd October, the French artillery fire started again with much strength. As early as

*A view of Fort Douaumont on 24th December 1916. General Séré de Rivières was far from knowing that the war could cause such devastation but Vaux and Douaumont resisted against modern artillery. Practically speaking, the situation turned in favour of the French by the end of august. On the 29th, General Hindenburg was appointed at the head of the German army and imposed a strict defensive position to Crown Prince's 5. Armee. At the same time, Genral Mangin prepared his offensive against Douaumont.*
*(IWM)*

*A piece of French heavy artillery in Belleville on 25th November 1916. The French shelling started on 21st October. 654 pieces poured on the area of Douaumont, including 20 heavy calibres, ranging from 270 to 400 mm. (IWM)*

18th October, it became a preliminary bombardment prior to an impending offensive. Three divisions took up positions on the first line (the 38th , 133rd, 74th D.I.). On 24th October, the French bombing intensified : it was an unprecedented shelling which brought chaos on the German lines.

*A French battalion CP during the counter-offensive in October 1916. Three fresh divisions from Bar-le-Duc and Saint-Dizier were about to strike, namely the 38th , 74th and 133rd D.I. (Author's coll.)*

# The recapture of Douaumont seen by the soldiers

Soldier Robert Laloum from the 321st R.I. has just learnt that his regiment would fight for the capture of Fort Douaumont. He recounts :

*"This is it, we'll be of those who are going to attack Fort Douaumont. We gather slowly, very slowly.*

*Our equipment is amazing. In addition to the regular equipment and our crammed cartridge pouch, we have two gas masks, a haversack for the biscuits, one for beef and chocolate, a third one for grenades, two bottles, one filled with wine and the other one with water, a blanket rolled in the tent sheet, a tool, two bags. We were all as large as a casket.*

*We left without enthusiasm. Verdun conjures up images of terror for all soldiers. All regiments had lost many men there. Against modern mechanical weapons, the foot soldier has no means of defence, hence his discouragement. The silence in the column when we left the town reveals more than anything else the anxiety of the troops. Each one thinks : " shall I die there or shall I come back?" Fear of death is the worst suffering that the Poilus has to endure."*

Soldier Roche from the 8th Battalion of the Colonial Infantry Regiment from Morocco describes the attack as it happened : *"The sight is horrendous, an ablaze cyclone fell on this land, excavated its soil, ripped it open, turned it upside down on every inch, nothing could resist our artillery and its terrible pounding. Lakes of mud and shell-holes are all that can be seen for miles around. Here and there, German corpses emerge, most of them horridly mangled up by pieces of shrapnel. Many comrades from preceding regiments also died on this battlefield. I run into a band of six Poilus from the regiment, lying on the ground, their eyes wide-open toward the sky, their faces darkened by the blast of shells."*

Sergeant Ducom, of 19/2 Engineer Company, recounts as he enters the fort : *"It was written that Fort Douaumont, on that night of 24th October 1916, was repulsively dirty and was filled with a disgusting smell. […] On the contrary, the Germans had extremely well organized this conquered place. Electrical lamps gave out bright light inside the fort, corridors were clean and the air is definitely not reeking."*

A Maxim machine-gun captured and used by French soldiers inside Fort Douaumont. It was the Colonial Infantry Regiment from Morocco who relieved Fort Douaumont, but they arrived a little late. That is why the foot soldiers from the 321st R.I. were the first to climb up the superstructures of Fort Douaumont. Nivelle clearly stated so in a letter joined to the regiment's war diary : "...On 24th October 1916, elements from the 321st R.I. were the first to enter by the eastern side of the fort and captured or chased away its defenders" .
(IWM)

At 11. 40 am, the French infantry went out of its parallels of departure. Some thick fog played in favour of the assailants as the German survivors were suddenly confronted to entire ranks of men stepping out of the fog at the last minute. Success was fast, except for the area around Fort Vaux.

In the area on the left, it was the Colonial Infantry Regiment from Morocco which had the privilege to recapture Fort Douaumont, a little after the due time though. The fort had been evacuated during the night, after a huge 400's shell had set a depot on fire. Unable to put it out, the garrison had left the fort. Early the next morning, Hauptmann Prollius and a small group of lost soldiers entered the fort. They inspected it and found it almost intact as the fire had gone out by itself. Prollius and his twenty men decided to defend the fort. He tried to get reinforcements in vain.

His last message, dated from 24th October at noon, stated : "*Weakened garrison will hold the*

*fort until the arrival of reinforcement.*" Three hours later, Mangin and his men arrived at the fort. It was recaptured by the French under the exact same circumstances as it had been taken in February 1916. The Germans made a mistake when they evacuated the fort during the bombardment and hoped they could re-enter it before the arrival of French troops.

The loss of Fort Douaumont was announced to the German nation on 26th October. It was a heavy blow to the morale of the population and to the German army as well. On 2nd November, Fort Vaux was abandoned by its defenders and,

*The quarries of Haudromont were strongly-organized by German troops and perfectly fortified. They were reached by the 11th R.I. on 24th October 1916. The first line trenches were abandoned, probably because of the strength of the French preliminary bombing. However, the inside of the quarries was strongly held by the Germans. After a harsh fight with grenades, the 11th R.I. managed to take the German garrison. (Ysec's coll.)*

*A navy piece of 240 mm at the Ravin des Grands Houyers near Fort Vaux. (Private coll.)*

*One of the entries of Fort Vaux during its recapture. Evacuated by the Germans because it had become too exposed, the fort was recaptured during the night of 2nd -3rd November 1916. Padre Sergeant Cheylan, 118th R.I., was given the following mission : "Instructions : Make a lot of noise to become targets for the soldiers, if there are some left in the fort. The men accept the mission without much enthusiasm [...] Here is the ditch. We hesitantly go down there. Silence is everywhere. Finally, we slide down the slope and we run into the patrol of the 298th ".*
*(IWM)*

on the same night, the French flag was hoisted on its devastated superstructures.

Finally, on 15th December, four French divisions entirely relieved both forts, pushing the Germans away, more than three kilometres north of Douaumont. They also relieved the villages of Louvemont and Bezonvaux. Success was complete and the lost grounds on the right bank were almost entirely regained. The Mort-Homme and Hill 304 would not be recaptured until 1917 though.

## A terrible toll

For Germany, the defeat was really significant. Despite amazing losses and a eight-month obstinate battle, it was an utter failure, Verdun did not surrender, the French army did not bleed to death. They were even able to help the British troops in the Somme, and then regain most of the

lost grounds. The losses were equal for both sides : 163,000 French dead against 143,000 Germans.

The first victim of this defeat was von Falkenhayn, replaced by the two war heroes of the Eastern Front, Hindenburg and Ludendorff. When they took command of the army, they found worn out soldiers, bogged down in deep depression. It would take at least a year to put them back on track. For the fist time since the outbreak of the war, some strong doubts concerning victory started weighing on the minds of the soldiers and the population.

For the French army, the victory in Verdun was tremendously important. It was the last time France was victorious without the Allies. Almost the entire army came and fought in Verdun, sometimes two or three times for some divisions. That is the reason why the battle of Verdun remains for the French the symbol of the First World War, if not the symbol of the French spirit.

*The ossuary in Douaumont in its primary temporary form. It is very small and cannot be compared to today's massive monument. Guns were put in front of the door. We can recognize a German piece of 77 mm in the foreground and an old French gun of Bange system behind it.*

*The ruins of Verdun photographed on 14th November 1916. Some houses remained miraculously intact but a lot of them were hit and many roofs apsed. Verdun could no longer be a town where troops could stay and rest, as they had done during the first two years of war. However, the citadel with impregnable walls remained a place where troops could set up temporary quarters.*

## Verdun after Verdun

Less famous than the first battle of Verdun in 1916, the limited offensive successfully carried out in 1917 by General Pétain deserves a few lines in any book about Verdun. After the recaptures of Fort Douaumont and Fort Vaux at the end of 1916, calm came back around Verdun but the front remained a dangerous and deadly area, around Besonvaux for instance, on the right bank. On the left bank of the Meuse river, the Germans still held the two heights that they had so much fought for, Mort-Homme hill and Hill 304.

In April 1917, Nivelle's offensive of the Chemin des Dames tragically failed and continuing the offensive in May led to a serious morale crisis and triggered many mutinies. To recover from such an unprecedented disaster, Nivelle was dismissed and replaced by the man who had managed to deal with the crisis in Verdun in February 1916, namely Philippe Pétain.

To raise the troops' morale, the new General-in-Chief slightly improved the conditions of

*German prisoners at Hill 304, photographed in August 1917 during the second battle of Verdun, the first offensive with limited objective launched by General Pétain. The attacks were meant to restore trusting bonds between the French soldiers, the army and the chiefs. Well-prepared, the attack was a success and allowed the French to recapture the hills of the left bank of the Meuse river, and to advance in the north of Douaumont. (Author's coll.)*

living of the Poilus. Moreover, they regained some confidence thanks to small victories with little losses, resulting from a perfect preparation. That was what happened with the second battle of Verdun. This offensive had a limited objective (the recapture of Mort-Homme and Hill 304) but much means were available : four army corps, 2,329 pieces of artillery, including 1,373 big calibres and 268 trench mortars.

*A Schneider short-distance 155 mm gun. An excellent and widely used weapon during the second battle of Verdun. (IWM)*

The Battle of Verdun

Inside of the Ossuary of Douaumont.
*Whoever, Passenger, go in and greet well low,
the Remains of the Heroes fallen for your salvation.*
Temporary ossuary of the Battle fields of Verdun (left bank and right bank).
Beginning of the Action of Douaumont, waiting for the definitive monument.

*View of the temporary ossuary in Douaumont where thousands of bones were gathered from the battlefield. Here is a description of the battlefield at the end of November 1916 which tells a lot on this macabre mission, given by J. Carafay, a stretcher-bearer from the 118th R.I. :
"In every shell-hole, there were one or more corpses, some were lying on their back, other on their stomach [...] There were human remnants and mangled limbs everywhere. We walk along an almost entirely filled up trench where we can see, here and there, an arm, a leg or a head coming out. It was even worse in the quarries of Vaux, said a priest who went down there yesterday. Over there, there were heaps of corpses".
(Ysec's coll.)*

The battle was short since it lasted from 20th -24th August 1917. However, it allowed the French to recapture Mort-Homme hill and the Hill 304. As a result, the French army regained almost all the positions they had lost with the German offensive of February 1916. The advance on the left bank forced the Germans to withdraw on the right. On the left bank, the front came to a standstill from Avocourt to Regnéville, from the northern slopes of Hill 304 to Mort-Homme hill. On the right bank, the front spread from Samogneux to Bezonvaux, through Beaumont.

However, the villages of Malancourt, Béthincourt, Forges, Haumont and the Bois des Caures remained in German hands. It represented very little on a map compared to all the means which had been at work for months.

That is how the battle of Verdun ended for the French troops. In 1918, the American soldiers would bravely fight on the flanks of the fortress, in Saint-Mihiel and in Argonne.

ILS N'ONT PAS PASSÉ

# NOTICE

To best visit the battlefields of Verdun and the Meuse area, it is recommended to bring some equipment : first of all, this helpful guide which
will put places in their historical background. You will also need a series
of IGN maps (by the National Geographical Institute) on a scale of 1 to
25,000. The maps of the Mort-Homme hill and Hill 304 indicate for
example the ancient location of trenches. As a matter of fact, the visitor
with very little time can get an interesting overall view of the battle
through the visits of Fort Douaumont and Fort Vaux, the Memorial in
Fleury and the underground citadel of Verdun. For those who wish to go
further in their approach of the battlefields, it is recommended to walk
along the way-marked footpaths. It is also possible to leave those paths
but it can be difficult and dangerous to walk through the forest because
of shell-holes and undetonated explosives. The visitor should be very
careful and should not trespass on forbidden grounds. Concerning the
battlefields in the Argonne and on the salient of Saint-Mihiel, way-
marked footpaths are more rare. In Vauquois, the visitor cannot walk into
the galleries without a guide from the Association des Amis de Vauquois
(a preservation society of the friends of Vauquois). Wearing a pair of boots
or good shoes is highly recommended.

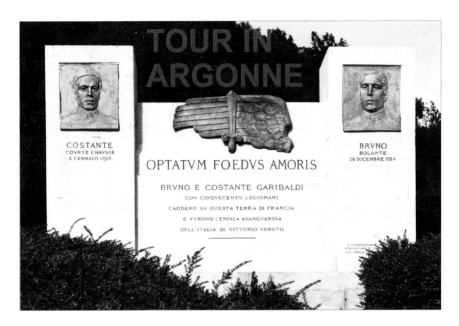

The best way is to start from Sainte-Menehould, above all if you drive from Paris. *To directly enter the atmosphere of the Argonne, follow the N3 road toward Verdun and turn left before Sainte-Menehould Exit, into the D85, toward Florent en Argonne.* On the right, you can see a huge national cemetery where thousands of men who fought in the Argonne were buried. *Keep following the D85 through the Valmy forest (the famous mill is a dozen kilometres west). When you are in Saint-Florent, drive down the Biesme valley.* As you drive out of the village, you drive by another national cemetery.

*The road goes down to Le Claon. Turn left into the D2.* When you arrive in the hamlet of Lachalade, you discover on your right a meadow which used to be the cemetery for Italian volunteers, killed alongside with the Garibaldi brothers, from 1914 to the beginning of 1915, before Italy entered the war as an ally of France. A monument is standing in the middle of the slope, with the bronze portraits of Bruno, the

*The monument honours the memory of the Garibaldi brothers, Costante and Bruno, as well as all the Italian volunteers who fought in the Argonne during winter 1914-15, before Italy became an ally. This monument was raised on a former Italian cemetery in Lachalade. (Ysec's coll.)*

*The shelters of the Crown Prince are one of the most visited sites in the Argonne forest and are really worth the visit. It looks like a village of bunkers and feel free to walk into the forest to discover all of them. (JL Kaluzko's coll.)*

*On the front of Verdun, the best way to see moving and rare vestiges is to walk to the sites. On top, the fountain of L'Homme-Mort in the town of Binarville, was erected to the memory of the king of Würtemberg by the 19. Reserve Division. (JL. Kaluzko's coll.)*
*Picture below. This shelter is located on the outskirts of the forest in Servon-Melzicourt. (Bohée's coll.)*

grand-son of the famous Garibaldi, killed in Bolante on 26th December 1914, and his brother Costante, killed in Courtes-Chausses ten days later, on 5th January 1915.

*Drive on northward along the D2.* The Four-de-Paris used to be a little hamlet in 1914 but was totally destroyed. Nothing remains except for the big cross on the right.

*Stay in the valley and drive on to La Harazée.* A national cemetery is located near the small chapel. If you walk along the path which leads to the cemetery, you run into a series of shelters which were hewn into the rock. The front was actually a few hundreds of meters north, in the forest.

*Then, drive to Vienne-le-Château and take the D 63 toward Bénarville.* As you drive up to the Bois de la Gruerie, you quickly see a big national cemetery on the left and an ossuary on the right. You are where the front was located, at the exact place where von Mudra launched some of his deadliest offensives against the French. If you turn left toward Servon-Melzicourt, you discover several monuments and individual tombstones, on both sides of the road. *Drive back to the D63 and head for Binarville.* At the entry of the town, a monument commemorates the 9th Cuirassiers.

*A war memorial dedicated to the Landwehr Infanterie Regiment 22, in the German military cemetery in Apremont. That unit belonged to the 16. Armeekorps of von Mudra. (Bohée's coll.)*

*Statue of Notre Dame la Gruerie, sculpted by soldier Hubert Briesacker from the Grenadier Regiment 123 from Ulm. That statue and a wooden Christ were found in a cemetery of the Bois-la-Gruerie. Today, they are exposed in the church of Vienne-le-Château. (Bohée's coll.)*

*When you are in Binarville, take the D 66 toward Apremont.* After the pond of Charleveau, a sign on the right indicates the position of the "Lost Battalion", an American unit who remained isolated there for several days in October 1918.

*In Apremont, take the road toward Varennes-en-Argonne,* a famous little town where King Louis XVI was arrested with his family on 21st June 1791. A huge American mausoleum stands in this town to commemorate the soldiers from Pennsylvania. A few meters away from there, the museum of Argonne is a must-see one.

All the aspects of the war in Argonne and in Vauquois are indeed depicted there, the war of mines for instance, through pictures and models. You can also see uniforms, weapons, and guns as well. Books about the region are on sale at the cash desk.

*The ossuary of the Argonne at Haute-Chevauchée, stands on the exact spot where Hill 285 used to be. In the foreground, you can see wooden benches for pilgrims. This interesting monument is like a History book : the four sides of the obelisk are covered with the names of all the allied units who served in the Argonne, including the air force. (JL. Kaluzko's coll.)*

*In Varennes, take the D38 toward the Four-de-Paris. On top of the slope, follow the dirt track (suitable for vehicles) on your right.* It opens onto a clearing. If you make a few steps away toward the North, you can see a lot of German concrete shelters. These are the shelters of the Crown Prince and are perfectly preserved. The entry is forbidden in the first on the left but if you walk deeper in the forest, you can enter and visit all the other ones. All the blockhouses are connected by deep trenches.

*Go back on the D38. At the following crossroads, turn left to drive into the road of the Haute-Chevauchée.* This is a nice road on the ridge of the Argonne massif. Many isolated tombs are indicated on the right. After a turn, you arrive at the famous Hill 285 where ruthless battles took place on 13th and 14th July 1915. A must-see ossuary stands on the left. It is an interesting monument for it lists the names of all the French, American, Italian regiments who fought in the Argonne. All the squadrons are also quoted. Behind it, there is a huge crater, the width and depth of which are really breathtaking. A little path winds between amazingly deep shell-holes, last testimonies of the underground war which took place there in 1915 and 1916.

On the first Sunday of July, a pilgrimage to commemorate the 100,000 dead of the Argonne's battles takes place in front of this ossuary, inaugurated by Poincaré in 1922.

*Current view of the location of Hill 285, very close to the ossuary of Haute-Chevauchée. The picture shows well-preserved German trenches. This ground was gained by the Germans on 13th July 1915 and was not relieved until the American attack in the Meuse and Argonne areas. (Simonin's coll.)*

If you walk on southward, you can see a French concrete shelter carrying a stele in memory of Lieutenant de Courson, killed in 1915.

This blockhouse represents the limit of the rear front. The first trenches leading to the front line started here.

*At the crossroads where a cross stands, it is better to turn right and head for Le Claon and the Biesme valley. From that hamlet, take the D2 on the left, toward the Islettes. A military cemetery can be seen at the entry of the village where you should join the N3. From there, you can either drive back to Sainte-Menehould to join the motorway to Verdun, or drive to Vauquois, via Clermont-en-Argonne and Neuvilly.*

*The cross of the Argonne, set back from the Haute-Chevauchée road and located amid remaining craters, commemorates the 150,000 soldiers who died in the Argonne, German and American soldiers included. (Simonin'scoll.)*

# THE AMERICANS IN THE MEUSE

A historical and tourist guide about Verdun and its area would be incomplete without a few words on the preponderant role of the American armies during the last months of the war. The Americans arrived on Verdun's front when the battles had calmed down, as early as 1917, and several divisions had their first fight there, alongside French units. It was later in September 1918 that a million of American soldiers fought there under solely American command.

The first massive attack was supervised by General Pershing and aimed at reducing the salient in Saint-Mihiel whose front had not moved since the tragic attack of the Woëvre in April 1915. The Americans had a lot of means to succeed in their mission : 660,000 men backed up by 1,400 planes and 3,010 pieces of artillery. They were all made in France as most planes were. It was really different from 1915 warfare...

The American strategy was quite plain: pincer attack of the salient and most efforts focused on the south with two army corps (I and IV US Corps). In the north, the 26th Division would focus on Vigneulles. The American preparations were too obvious though and on the eve of the attack, the defenders were ready for the evacuation of the salient.

On 12th September, following masterly primary artillery assaults, the Americans launched their attack. The success was tremendous, all the more since the Germans had already evacuated their heavy artillery. At the close of the day, some American units had reached the objective of the day after! During the night of 12th-13th September, the Americans intensified the offensive because an air reconnaissance told them that the Germans were hurriedly drawing back toward the North-East. At 6 am, on 13th September, the American soldiers of the 26th Division joined the I Corps : 16,000 Germans were captured as well as 443 pieces of all calibre artillery.

The Americans of the First Army only lost 7,000 men, dead and wounded. Right after this great success, Pershing's army headed for the North, in the Argonne. They were ordered a major mission : to breakthrough the front in this area and head for Sedan to cut off the German communication links, which would engender a real disaster for Ludendorff's troops fighting in Flandres and Artois.

To ward off the threat, the Germans fortified all the hillocks situated between the Argonne and the Meuse. They hoped each top would be as impregnable as the Butte de Vauquois. They gathered five divisions on the front line and twelve reserve ones were standing nearby.

Pershing had eight divisions on the front line and five reserve ones. The German supremacy was purely theoretical since the American divisions counted twice more men than the German ones.

On 26th September 1918, the American attack started promptly, except for Montfaucon, but it slowed down on the day after. In a fit of anger, and he was quite famous for that, Clemenceau blamed the Americans for all evils, and accused them of jeopardizing the allied victory.

It was true that Pershing's advance was checked : in four days, they had only advanced on twelve kilometres and losses were huge. By 4th October, the Americans had already lost 75,000 men. On the German side too, the troops were quickly worn out and Ludendorff had to send 17 divisions to the first line to maintain the front.

On 4th October, the battle intensified but it was not until the end of the month that the Americans broke through Hindenburg's line. That was the beginning of the end for the Germans. During the night of 10th -11th November, the Meuse river was crossed in Stenay. Germany surrendered a few hours later. The American victory was really impressive but claimed 117,000 lives

# THE AMERICAN TOUR

*This picture and the one on page 88 show the American cemetery in Romagne-sous-Montfaucon, the most important one in France. Soldiers who were decorated with the highest american military award, the "Medal of honour", are recognizable by their golden star on the cross. (JL Kaluzko's coll.)*

The best place to start the American tour is Varennes-en-Argonne. *After admiring the monument dedicated to Pennsylvania, near the Museum of Argonne, take the D 946 toward Apremont, then turn right and take the D 998 toward Romagne-sous-Montfaucon.* There is a sign indicating the American cemetery. The entry of the necropolis is wonderful. On the south side of the hill spread 15,000 Carrara marble tombstones till a chapel that overhangs the biggest American cemetery in Europe. The lawn, the tombs, the trees and the buildings are neatly looked after. Opposite the chapel, on the north side of the hill, stands the house of the curator where you can come in for some information on American necropolises in France and Europe. The marble entry hall is really worth seeing.

*Leave the cemetery and head for the East, to Cunel and then Nantillois.* At the entry of the village, a German cemetery is indicated on the left, a few hundred kilometres away from there. *Drive on till Montfaucon where a huge column*

*rises with a statue of liberty on it.* Built in 1938, this column is composed of 235 stairs. From the top, you can see for miles around, including Vauquois, Hill 304 and Mort-Homme.

The ruins of the church are the only remnants of the old village of Montfaucon, where the Germans had set up a concrete observatory that can still be visited today. *From Montfaucon, take the D15 toward Avocourt and then Hill 304.* Do not forget that other American monuments can be found near Saint-Mihiel, on the Butte de Montsec for instance.

*A shellproof observatory built on the ruins of the church on the Butte de Montfaucon. The place offers visitors a beautiful view for miles around. The huge column with the statue of liberty on it, is composed of 235 stairs. (JL Kaluzko's coll.)*

# VAUQUOIS

*Whether you are in Varennes or in Clermont, you need to go to Boureuilles first in order to get to Vauquois.* When you drive on the D 946, you clearly understand the tactical importance of Vauquois in the East, and the Hill 285 in the Argonne massif in the West. In order to walk on Varennes, the French army had to take Vauquois. The unfortunate attempt in Boureuilles made by two colonial infantry regiments on 17th February 1915 is an epitome of that.

*When you are in Boureuilles, take the D 212 toward Vauquois.* At the entry of the new village, you can either leave your car and walk up by an impressively steep path, or drive on and park your car on the left as it is indicated. From the parking lot, it is quite easy to reach the top of the hillock. The place is very neatly looked after by the dynamic *Association of the Friends of Vauquois and its area*, founded in 1985 by M. Parent.

On the last step which leads to the top, you can see a huge shell-hole which dates back to 14th May 1916. The whole hillock is devastated by mines. There is nothing left from the village as it was before 1914 and no other place, from the North Sea to Switzerland, conveys so vividly the tremendous violence of that war. The sight in Vauquois is really stupefying. On some days of the year, visits of the French and German galleries are organized by the friends of Vauquois.

To make enquiries, please contact :

Les Amis de Vauquois,
Hôtel de Ville,
55120 Clermont-sur-Argonne
Phone: 03 29 87 41 15

# THE ÉPARGES

The admirers of Maurice Genevoix should spend at least half a day in the Éparges area. The ridge in itself deserves a full visit but the whole area is interesting for the readers of *Ceux de 14* : the Trench of Calonne, Mesnil-sous-les-Côtes, Mouilly, Amblonville farm, etc. .

*As you leave Verdun by the south, take the D 964 to Saint-Mihiel. The road goes along the Meuse river and the canal de l'Est. After Génicourt, turn left into the D 21 toward Rupt-en-Woëvre.* There, you enter the world of Maurice Genevoix. In Rupt, you can find on the right a national cemetery with the graves of the soldiers killed between 1914 and 1915. In front of the town hall stands a 120 long Bange system gun. It is a typical piece of artillery from 1914-15. You can see the little wedges on the wheels which were necessary to aim properly when the terrain was unstable.

*On the Éparges ridge, one of the numerous shell holes left by the mine warfare, when both adversaries fought to hold the top. (Ysec's coll.)*

*A 120 mm long-distance gun of Bange system in front of the town hall in Rupt. It is a typical weapon from the beginning of the war. (JL Kaluzko's coll.)*

*Map of the Éparges, according to the pedestrian tour devised by the Memorial of Fleury. We advise you to get as many itineraries as you can since they are all informative. Keys on the map :*
*1. Point X, monument for the 302th R.I. and great view on Woëvre plain.*
*2. Mine-holes.*
*3. Point C, monument "Du Coq" erected in memory of the 12th D.I.*
*4. Old communication trench and concrete German shelter (aid post)*
*5. View on the German lines in Combres.*
*6. Monument erected to the glory of the Engineer soldiers. (see picture below)*
*7. Cemetery called du Trottoir (see on next page)*
*8. The shelter of the Crown Prince.*
*9. Monument to the 106th R.I. , Maurice Genevoix's unit. (Ysec's coll.)*

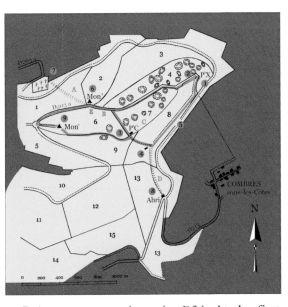

*Drive on eastward on the D21.* At the first crossroads, a choice has to be made : on the right, you go to the village of Mouilly where Genevoix spent a lot of time when not on the front. If you drive straight on, you drive by Amblonville's farm which is often quoted in Genevoix's book. By the D 21, you quickly arrive at the trench of Calonne, a narrow straight road marked out in the middle of the forest by a royal intendant. The 106th R.I. in which Genevoix served, spent a lot of days there when in reserve. The road is bordered with underground shelters. (the front was really close). *To really feel the 1914-15 period, you should drive down to Mesnil-sous-les-Côtes, then reach the village of Éparges via the Longeau valley.* Above the Éparges, the very last village that remained in French hands until 1918, you can see three impressive hillocks. The first is called the Montgirmont and was French in 1914. Separated by a valley called the Ravin de la Mort, the Éparges

ridge rises. It remained German till February 1915. Behind the ridge, a height called Combres was also in German hands.

Before February 1915, the French lines barely reached the flank of the Éparges ridge, where the cemetery du Trottoir is now located. That is the place where many soldiers died during the battles of 1915. The 16th gravestone of the first row on the right belongs to Genevoix's best friend, Robert Porchon.

Leaving the cemetery, the most courageous ones can climb up to the top of the ridge, by the small tracks leading to the top. It has to be said that it is a tiring and challenging walk : it proves the amazing deed French soldiers accomplished in February 1915. It may be wiser to take your car to go to the first monument dedicated to the 106th R.I.

Wooden signs are there to give explanations on the battle. Several way-marked paths enable the visitor to reach different monuments which stand along the way to the top of the ridge, amid shell-holes and huge craters. When you are on

*The cemetery du Trottoir, at the bottom of the Éparges ridge. Most soldiers buried there were killed during the battles of 1915. The tombstone of Robert Porchon can be found there. He was Maurice Genevoix's best friend and one of the heroes in Ceux de 14. (JL. Kaluzko's coll.)*

*Another view of the craters on the Éparges ridge. (Ysec's coll.)*

*View dating back to 1920 and showing the "shelter of the Crown Prince" at the bottom of the ridge, near Combres. It was held by the Germans. The current state of the bunker has worsened though. (Ysec's coll.)*

the road, the following monument is dedicated to the engineering soldiers. To go to point X which overhangs the entire Woëvre plain, the path winds around craters. From the point X, tracks lead you to the monument "du Coq" and to several German concrete shelters since the eastern side of the ridge could never be conquered by the French. The biggest bunker is naturally called "the shelter of the Crown Prince".

# THE LEFT BANK

Roads are not very good to go to the battlefields of the left bank. Hill 304 and the Mort-Homme attract less tourists than the right bank

COMBRES. — Entrance of the german tunnels acceding to the Eparges'crest. - Classed as historical monument.

ILS N'ONT PAS PASSE

The Mort-Homme monument shows a dead Frenchman wrapped in his shroud, holding the French flag, standing across the road to stop the invaders. The sentence "they did not pass" talks by itself. Even if the Germans did not manage to gain ground beyond the top of the Mort-Homme, they remained there until the offensive of General Guillaumat on 20th August 1917. (Ysec's coll.)

because there are no forts here. However, Hill 304 is a place filled with emotion.

*In Verdun, take the D 964 until Bras-sur-Meuse. When you arrived there, turn on the left toward Charny, then follow the D38 till Cumières, via Marre.*

The visitor should stop in Cumières, a village which was entirely destroyed in 1916. Even when you walk away into the forest, it is difficult to find a single remnant of wall. Several forest paths enable the visitor to walk safely into the Mort-Homme forest. You can run into entries of underground passages, shelters, tunnels. No need to say that it is very dangerous to penetrate there.

*It is better to get your car and head for Chattancourt to reach the top of Mort-Homme*

*The path of Hill 304.*
*Keys :*

*1.location of the German first line in June 1916.*
*2. Isolated tombstone of Sergeant Louis Courrier.*
*3. Very steep slopes of the Ravin du Petit Hoyau.*
*4. Former Bois Camard. In 1916, the Hill 304 was far less wooded than today.*
*5. Isolated tombstone of Pierre Lumret, killed in 1916.*
*6. Rest area, on the former southern end of Bois Pamard.*
*7. Delépine monument, at the far end of the position called "Bec de Canard".*
*8. Road leading to Hill 304 monument.*
*9. Path of Hill 304*
*10. Isolated grave stone of Joseph Girard, killed on 14th June 1940.*
*(Ysec map)*

*hill.* The first road on the right leads to Mort-Homme national cemetery. The second on the right leads to Mort-Homme itself. On top of the hill, you can see various monuments including that of the 40th D.I. The most famous one bears *"Ils n'ont pas passé"* on it, meaning *"they did not pass"*.

Now, Mort-Homme hill is covered with forests whereas only small clusters of trees stretched on its slopes before the 1916's offensive.

Go back to Chattancourt and take the D38 till Esnes-en-Argonne. Then, take the D18 toward Montfaucon.

On the way to Montfaucon, you come across several monuments on your right, including one which is dedicated to the defenders of Verdun in June 1940.

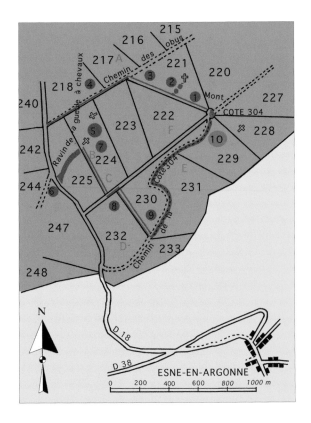

98

Once you entered the forest, turn on the right to reach Hill 304. The straight and narrow road disappears into a dark path lined up with black fir-trees.

The view is really impressive as you come closer to the monument to the memory of the 10,000 dead soldiers of Hill 304. It rises at the end of the path, in the middle of a little roundabout. From there, you can walk around the hill from a path that will make you discover the location of the German first lines in June 1916 and several isolated French tombstones.

After the visit, drive back to Esnes-en-Argonne. Before arriving in the village, turn right to get to the national cemetery where many soldiers from the fierce battles of Hill 304 are buried. Then, you can drive to Avocourt. The woods surrounding the north of the village are still filled with trenches. From Avocourt, it is easy to reach Vauquois via Buanthe valley where an astonishing series of French small blockhouses can be seen.

*The monument dedicated to the 10,000 dead of Hill 304. It is precisely located on Hill 304, not very far from the German first line in June 1916. (JL. Kaluzko's coll.)*

# VERDUN

The town of Verdun naturally deserves a complete visit.

The underground citadel has been entirely restored thanks to the efforts of the Office du Tourisme (tourist information office) of Verdun and this is probably the most impressive military monument in town.

Moreover, there are a lot of monuments you can visit in Verdun. The largest national cemetery is called "Faubourg Pavé" with 5,722 graves. Its entry is ornated with several pieces of French and German artillery. You can also find graves in the civilians'cemetery and in two other military necropolises of Bevaux and Glorieux, the last name referring to Verdun's suburb where the Voie Sacrée used to end.

The monument dedicated to Victory and its semi-circular crypt, can be visited from Easter to 11th November. The upper town, with the cathedral and the banks of the Meuse, is worth seeing too. The World Peace Centre in the former archbishop's palace, hosts some interesting exhibitions about WW1 but is not entirely dedicated to the battle of Verdun in 1916.

In June and July, the association called "Connaissance de la Meuse" (Knowledge on the Meuse area) organizes a wonderful son et lumière show retracing the battle. It takes place on Friday and Saturday nights, at 9.30 pm. Reservations should be made at the following phone number : 03 29 84 50 00. The show is set near the town, in a clearing located on the way to Nancy.

Verdun is the ideal place to start a tour of all the battlefields in the area, thanks to its central location and its good accommodation. Each year, more sites are opened to the public like for instance the Maguerre camp or the concrete tank of a German 380 mm gun.

# THE RIGHT BANK

*Leave Verdun by the RN 3. A little after the Bois des Hospices, turn left into the D 913 toward Tavannes and Fort Vaux.* At the first major crossroads, a road on the right leads to Fort Vaux, another on the left to Douaumont and Fleury. You may also leave your car on the rest area and walk along the path to Tavannes. Fort Tavannes, a couple of meters away from here, is now in ruins. As it was already very old in 1916, it played a minor role during the battle, all the more since it did not even have armoured armament. However, Tavannes tunnel was tremendously important as it was entirely bombproof, even against the heaviest shells. Located only a few steps away from the front line, thousands of men stationed there. Although they were sheltered from the German artillery, men were nevertheless submitted to promiscuity and poison gas whiffs which caused the conditions of living to be unbearable. It was by the way in that very tunnel that one of the worst tragedies of the bat-

Shelter 320, down the national necropolis of Douaumont. The scars left by violent artillery fires can still be seen on the ground.
On page 100, two generals who made themselves a name in Verdun. On the left, General von Falkenhayn, commander-in-chief of the German army and instigator of the offensive against Verdun. His failure caused his dismissal. On the left, wearing a horizon-blue uniform, General Pétain was the victorious man of the battle. He saved the town whereas the situation was desperate. When the defeated French army of the Chemin des Dames needed a saviour, he was promoted general-in-chief, in May 1917. (Ysec's coll.)

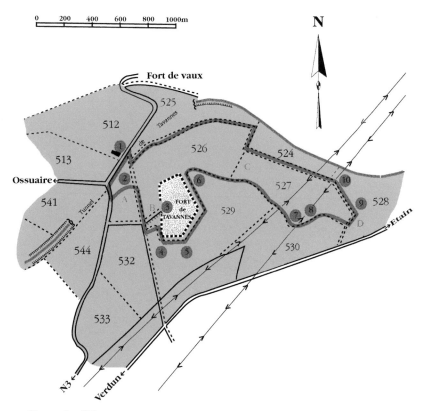

The path of Tavannes.

*The path of Tavannes.*
*Keys :*
*1. Shelter for the battery of the tunnel, built in 1888.*
*2. Twenty recesses for ammunitions dating from the same era.*
*3. Fort Tavannes. Deprived of any armoured armament.*
*4. Blockhouse for MG dating back to 1917.*
*5. and 6. Pamart Casemates.*
*7. Shelter LLM1 dating back to 1907.*
*8. Entrenchments.*
*9. Battery called " Mardi Gras" 10. Shelter for the searchlight*

tle took place. The explosion of a grenade depot engendered a real slaughter among the men of the 18th and 24th R.I. on 4th September 1916, claiming more than 500 lives.

*After visiting the surroundings of Tavannes, take your car and head northward, toward Fort Vaux.* The road goes down a little valley and a path on the right leads to the Monument "des Fusillés" of Tavannes, a monument dedicated to 16 Resistance fighters fire squaded by the Germans in 1944. On the north side of the valley, a path leads to La Laufée works, a small fortification which was to become important after the fall of Fort Vaux. Several tracks in the forest lead to some important places of the battle, namely the battery of Damloup, the Fond de la Horgne, etc.

To finish, the dead-end road leads to Fort Vaux. The visit fee is really cheap. The whole epic story of Commandant Raynal is vividly detailed thanks to learned guides. Most parts of the fort are open to the public, including Bourges casemate in the north-west angle of the fort, and its 75mm gun.

*Drive back to where you came from and when you arrive at Tavannes crossroads, turn right toward Fleury.* You set foot on the battlefield of June and July 1916, when the last desperate

*The Casemates of Fort Vaux. On top, the little bomb-proof dome is an observatory. (Ysec's coll.)*

*A retractable turret from Fort Douaumont for two short 75 mm guns. (Ysec's coll.)*

*View from the top of Fort Douaumont in direction of the ossuary, the lighthouse of which stands out against the background. (Ysec's coll.)*

*A one-hour walk on the path of Souville (green marks)*
1. *Start of the path said "du Tacot", down the memorial of Fleury.*
2. *Crossroads of Sainte Fine chapel and Monument du Lion, erected by the former soldiers of the 130th D.I. It indicates the position of the furthest German advance (which was not all true since the Germans reached the top of Fort Souville).*
3. *Monument to the memory of André Maginot, future minister of War, wounded in Verdun.*
4. *Pamart Casemate.*
5. *155 mm gun turret and observation dome.*
6. *Path of Souville, one of the access to the battlefield in 1916.*
7. *Wartime entry of Fort Souville.*
8. *Boyau des Carrières, a communication trench which led the soldiers of Verdun to the front of Vaux.*
9. *Two Pamart Casemates.*
*On the right page : The path of Fleury.*
1. *Layout of the ancient railroad, a 60 cm railway.*
2. *Poudrière de Fleury, taken by the Germans on 11th July 1916.*
2b. *Grave of Caporal Machine-gunner Rachel.*

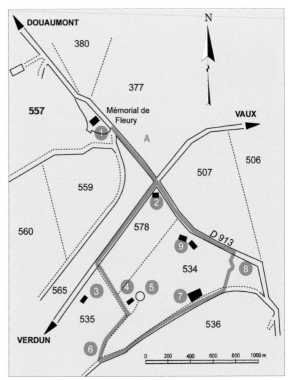

German assaults were made against Verdun. At Fort Souville, you can have access to Pamart casemate on which a viewpoint indicator can be found. Fort Souville is only a dozen of kilometres away but cannot be visited. It is indeed in the worst conditions and risks of collapsing are too important.

*A couple of meters away from there, you can notice at the crossroads of the D 112 the Monument "au Lion de Souville".* It is supposed to indicate the furthest German advance on Verdun, on 26th June 1916. Actually, the Crown Prince's men managed to go even closer to Verdun on 11th July, namely on the top of Fort Souville and in the Ravin de la Poudrière

If you drive on toward Douaumont, you soon arrive at the Memorial of Fleury, the most important museum on the battle of Verdun. The memorial is an exceptional place in many

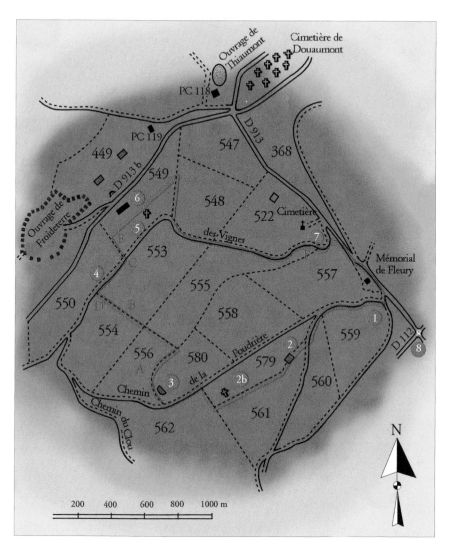

aspects. First, it was built in 1967 by the Comité National du Souvenir (a national comity dedicated to remembrance) on the former train-station of Fleury, an important location during the battle. The collections are very precious for they are composed of personal donations made by the soldiers of Verdun. Scholars can also find there an important research department.

As the visitor enters the museum, he is struck by the presence of two planes hanging from the

3. D works or Morpion.
4. Ravin des Vignes.
5. Stele to the memory of Captain Cazalis de Fondouce, killed on 23rd June 1916.
6. Quatre Cheminées Shelter.
7. Chapel of the destroyed village of Fleury.
8. Lion de Souville monument.

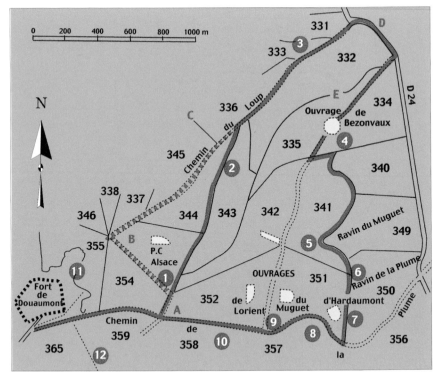

The path of Hardaumont.
1. The Command Post "Alsace" is 400 meters north.
2. Former outskirt of the Bois d'Hardaumont.
3. The Fond du Loup, a relief road for the German troops.
4. Bezonvaux works.
5 & 6. Ravin du Muguet and Ravin de la Plume.
7. Remnants of Hardaumont works.
8. Ravin des Grands Houyers.
9. Lorient works and Muguet works.
10. Ravin de la Fosse Côte.
11. Eastern turret and battery of Fort Douaumont.
12. Infantry shelter.

ceiling : a Nieuport 17 and a Fokker E III. These are two perfect full-scale models hanging above a life-size reconstruction of the battlefield in 1916.

The upper gallery retraces the battle in 1916 and puts it back into context. The events of 1914-15 are thus recalled as well as the French offensives of summer 1917. Maps, pictures, pieces of uniforms, equipments and models perfectly convey and recreate the atmosphere of WW1.

The lower gallery is specifically devoted to army movements and actions. Many weapons can be seen from the Lebel riffle to a 75 mm gun, without forgetting the Maxim machine gun, etc. One of the biggest pieces is probably a Berliet lorry from the Voie Sacrée.

Behind the reconstructed battlefield, a huge map on the wall allows the visitor to follow the process of the battle with comments in many different languages.

You can also attend a screening of films from the 1910's. To finish, a gift shop sells many souvenirs and an important collection of books about the battle.

From the esplanade of the Memorial, several paths lead to the ossuary of Douaumont and the Ravin de La Caillette for instance.

*Go back to your car and stop at the ossuary of Douaumont.* There rest the remnants of 130,000 French soldiers to whom we could add the 14,637 men buried in front of the ossuary.

They did not all die in Verdun but also in the other battles of the Meuse area, in Woëvre plain for instance.

The ossuary can be visited and you may also walk up to the top of the lighthouse where the view on the battlefield is exceptional. The proximity of the Memorial of Fleury is striking as we know it took the Germans four months to cover

*The path of Froideterre*
*1. Ossuary and national necropolis of Douaumont*
*2. Ruins of Thiaumont works, taken and lost a dozen times.*
*3. C.P. 118.*
*4. CP. 119.*
*4b. Toward Y and X concrete entrenchments.*
*5. F.T.1 and F.T.2 shelters.*
*6. Froideterre works, besieged on 23rd June 1916 but relieved on the same day.*
*7. Concrete shelters.*
*8. Quatre-Cheminées Shelter.*
*9. Monument to the glory of the Jewish volunteers who died in Verdun.*
*10. Monument to the 4th Mixed Regiment of Zouave Riflemen.*

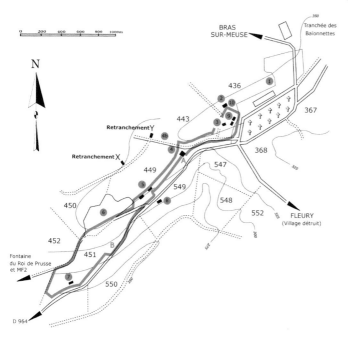

*A typical view of the ossuary in Douaumont and the rows of crosses of the huge necropolis. (Ysec's coll.)*

*The ossuary in Douaumont seen from the area of Thiaumont. (Ysec's coll.)*

*The peculiar red colour reflected by the stained-glass windows of the ossuary's gallery. (Ysec's coll.)*

the distance between Douaumont and Fleury, in 1916. Apart from that, the ground is now covered with trees and has nothing to do with the place it used to be in 1916 or even prior to the war.

From the ossuary, you can go to Fort Douaumont. The guided tour lasts for about 45 minutes and is a must-see. Despite the pounding the fort was submitted to for months, the interior is in remarkable conditions. Several turrets can be visited, including a retractable one for 155 mm gun. A walled up gallery contains the

remnants of several dozens of German soldiers killed during the battle.

*Go back to the ossuary and turn right toward the "tranchée des baïonnettes",* the trench of the bayonets. As opposed to what the legend says, the men of the 137th R.I. who rest there, were not buried alive. As it was often the case during the battle, the bodies were buried in a trench and the place was indicated with their guns. And the rest of it is but a legend.

*You can go back toward the ossuary, drive by it and take the D913b toward the Meuse.*

The vestiges of several fortifications can still be seen and even visited, namely the Quatre Cheminées shelter as well as Thiaumont works, Command Post 119, Froideterre works, etc.

If you have some more time, hiking is of course the best way to visit the sites. You can also visit the northern area of the battlefield, in particular the famous Bois des Caures and Colonel Driant's Command Post.

*The trench called "Des Baïonnettes" is a particular memorial built with American funds right after the war. Today, nothing remains from the riffles and bayonets which used to be here. The story about the men buried alive remains unconfirmed. Dead soldiers of the 137th R.I. were indeed buried there but not buried alive. The location of the bodies was marked with the soldiers'riffles, a common custom in Verdun where it was almost impossible to bury all the bodies decently. (Ysec's coll.)*

*Close-up on the Jewish memorial of Douaumont to the memory of Jewish French soldiers and volunteers.*
*(Ysec's coll.)*

# PRACTICAL GUIDE
## MUSEUMS AND PERMANENT EXHIBITIONS

Here are some helpful details about must-see places mentioned in the guide :

Sainte-Menehould : Viard-Morel Museum of the Argonne, place du général Leclerc, 51800 Sainte-Menehould. A room is entirely devoted to WW1, with an impressive post-cards collection. Opening hours vary according to seasons. Make sure you call the tourist information office (syndicat d'initiative) before visiting : 03 26 60 85 83.

Varennes-en-Argonne : Museum of Argonne. Open everyday from Easter to All Saints' day, from 2 pm to 6 pm. In June and July, it is also open in the morning from 10 am to 12 am. This museum is really worth visiting. Phone number : 03 29 80 71 14.

Raymond Poincaré Museum, Clos Raymond-Poincaré, Sampigny, 55300 Saint-Mihiel. Open everyday from 1st May to 11th November, from 2 pm to 6pm. Can be visited in winter by appointment only. Please call : 03 29 90 70 50. This museum is set in the summer house of president Raymond Poincaré which was located a few kilometres away from the German lines.

Town Hall of Souilly, 55220 Souilly. It is not a museum but it is the place where Pétain set up his Headquarters. A room reminding of this glorious past can be visited. It is better to make an appointment first. Please call : 03 29 80 52 76.

Verdun, the underground citadel. Opening hours vary according to seasons but it is generally open at regular hours, with a lunch break, off season. For further details, please call the tourist office : 03 29 86 14 18.

Fort Douaumont. This symbol of the battle of Verdun is open all day from 15th February to 12th December. For further details on exact hours, please call Verdun's tourist office.

Fort Vaux : same opening hours as Fort Douaumont.

Ossuary in Douaumont : Open from 1st March to 30th November, from 9 am. Closed off season between 12 and 2 pm. Closed around 5 to 6.30 pm according to season. Phone number : 03 29 84 54 81.

Office du Tourisme de Verdun, place de la Nation, 55100 Verdun. Phone number : 03 29 86 14 18.

## MILITARY CEMETERIES IN THE MEUSE

### French national necropolises :

French military cemeteries are particularly numerous in the Meuse area, since there are thirty-nine of them. We shall only quote here the most important ones

Douaumont : 14,637 graves and the remnants of 130,000 men in one ossuary;

Verdun, Faubourg-Pavé : 4,887 graves;

Bras-sur-Meuse : 4,226 graves;

Verdun, Glorieux : 3,261 graves;

Esnes-en-Argonne : 3,587 graves and the remnants of 3,046 men in two ossuaries;

Verdun, Bevaux : 3,107 graves;

Bar-le-Duc : 3,065 graves and the remnants of 63 men in two ossuaries;

Vauquois : 2,400 graves and the remnants of 1,972 men in two ossuaries;

Les Islettes : 2,227 graves;

Marbotte : 2,185 graves and 388 bodies in an ossuary;

Rembercourt-aux-Pots : 2,146 graves and the remnants of 3,357 French soldiers in two ossuaries and the bodies of 4,395 German soldiers in one ossuary;

Commercy : 2,119 graves;

Lachalade (in Argonne) : 2,004 graves;

Avocourt : 1,846 graves;

Dugny : 1,814 graves and 124 bodies in an ossuary;

Chattancourt : 1,713 graves;

Les Éparges : 1,660 graves;

Vadelaincourt : 1,645 graves;

Saint-Mihiel : 1,513 graves and the remnants of 2,005 men in three ossuaries.

## American military cemeteries :

After the war, the Americans gathered most graves and families had 60% of the bodies sent back to the United States. That is the reason why a single one American cemetery is to be found in the Meuse area, in Romagne-sous-Montfaucon. With 14,000 graves, this is the most important one in Europe, twice as big as the cemetery in Saint-Laurent-sur-Mer where G.I.'s from the D-day are buried. That proves how harsh the offensive in Meuse-Argonne was for the American army. Another American cemetery can be found in Thiaucourt-Regniéville, in Meurthe-et-Moselle.

## The German military cemeteries :

They are numerous and the most important ones in the Argonne (battles in 1914-16 and 1918) are the followings :

Servon-Melzicourt : more than 10,000 bodies, including 6,500 in ossuaries.

Apremont : 1,111 graves.

Cheppy : 2,341 graves and 3,789 bodies in an ossuary.

In the north of Verdun, you can find German cemeteries in Ville-devant-Chaumont, Azannes, Romagne-sous-les-Côtes, Damvillers, Lissey, Peuvillers, Mangiennes, Merles-sur-Loison. Around Saint-Mihiel, the most important German cemeteries are :

Vaux-les-Palameix : about 5,500 bodies.

Saint-Mihiel : 6,000 bodies.

Thiaucourt-Regniéville (in Meurthe-et-Moselle) : more than 10,000 bodies. This is also the town where is located the American cemetery of the offensive against the salient of Saint-Mihiel.

## HIKING TOURS ON THE BATTLEFIELD.

Thanks to the Memorial of Verdun in Fleury, many way-marked paths are available for visitors. You can get free brochures of these tours at the Memorial or in Verdun's tourist office. The brochure is a A4 sheet folded in two parts, with a map of the path inside and historical comments about the vestiges you will see, on both sides. This is valuable information about the battlefield but our guide will be very helpful to truly understand the way battles took place.

Most sectors of the front are covered by these brochures and it would be too long to list them here since there are 12 brochures (two about the left bank, nine on the right bank and one for the Éparges). The latest brochure deals with Tavannes.

Maps and plans that illustrate this part of the guide are inspired from these excellent and informative brochures.

Ysec Éditions
BP 405
27404 Louviers Cedex
Tél. : 02 32 50 26 74

Achevé d'imprimer dans l'Union européenne - Mai 2018